U·X·L
Encyclopedia
of Science

U·X·L
Encyclopedia
of Science

Second Edition
Volume 8: P-Ra

Rob Nagel, Editor

U·X·L

GALE GROUP

THOMSON LEARNING

Detroit • New York • San Diego • San Francisco
Boston • New Haven, Conn. • Waterville, Maine
London • Munich

U·X·L
Encyclopedia of Science
Second Edition

Rob Nagel, *Editor*

Staff

Elizabeth Shaw Grunow, *U•X•L Editor*

Julie Carnagie, *Contributing Editor*

Carol DeKane Nagel, *U•X•L Managing Editor*

Thomas L. Romig, *U•X•L Publisher*

Shalice Shah-Caldwell, *Permissions Associate (Pictures)*

Robyn Young, *Imaging and Multimedia Content Editor*

Rita Wimberley, *Senior Buyer*

Pamela A. E. Galbreath, *Senior Art Designer*

Michelle Cadorée, *Indexing*

GGS Information Services, *Typesetting*

On the front cover: Nikola Tesla with one of his generators, reproduced by permission of the Granger Collection.

On the back cover: The flow of red blood cells through blood vessels, reproduced by permission of Phototake.

Library of Congress Cataloging-in-Publication Data

U-X-L encyclopedia of science.—2nd ed. / Rob Nagel, editor
    p.cm.
   Includes bibliographical references and indexes.
   Contents: v.1. A-As — v.2. At-Car — v.3. Cat-Cy — v.4. D-Em — v.5. En-G — v.6. H-Mar — v.7. Mas-O — v.8. P-Ra — v.9. Re-St — v.10. Su-Z.
   Summary: Includes 600 topics in the life, earth, and physical sciences as well as in engineering, technology, math, environmental science, and psychology.
   ISBN 0-7876-5432-9 (set : acid-free paper) — ISBN 0-7876-5433-7 (v.1 : acid-free paper) — ISBN 0-7876-5434-5 (v.2 : acid-free paper) — ISBN 0-7876-5435-3 (v.3 : acid-free paper) — ISBN 0-7876-5436-1 (v.4 : acid-free paper) — ISBN 0-7876-5437-X (v.5 : acid-free paper) — ISBN 0-7876-5438-8 (v.6 : acid-free paper) — ISBN 0-7876-5439-6 (v.7 : acid-free paper) — ISBN 0-7876-5440-X (v.8 : acid-free paper) — ISBN 0-7876-5441-8 (v.9 : acid-free paper) — ISBN 0-7876-5775-1 (v.10 : acid-free paper)

   1. Science-Encyclopedias, Juvenile. 2. Technology-Encyclopedias, Juvenile. [1. Science-Encyclopedias. 2. Technology-Encyclopedias.] I. Title: UXL encyclopedia of science. II. Nagel, Rob.
Q121.U18 2001
503-dc21
                                          2001035562

Printed in the United States of America

10 9 8 7 6 5 4 3 2 1

Table of Contents

Contents

Reader's Guide

Demystify scientific theories, controversies, discoveries, and phenomena with the *U•X•L Encyclopedia of Science,* Second Edition.

This alphabetically organized ten-volume set opens up the entire world of science in clear, nontechnical language. More than 600 entries—an increase of more than 10 percent from the first edition—provide fascinating facts covering the entire spectrum of science. This second edition features more than 50 new entries and more than 100 updated entries. These informative essays range from 250 to 2,500 words, many of which include helpful sidebar boxes that highlight fascinating facts and phenomena. Topics profiled are related to the physical, life, and earth sciences, as well as to math, psychology, engineering, technology, and the environment.

In addition to solid information, the *Encyclopedia* also provides these features:

- "Words to Know" boxes that define commonly used terms
- Extensive cross references that lead directly to related entries
- A table of contents by scientific field that organizes the entries
- More than 600 color and black-and-white photos and technical drawings
- Sources for further study, including books, magazines, and Web sites

Each volume concludes with a cumulative subject index, making it easy to locate quickly the theories, people, objects, and inventions discussed throughout the *U•X•L Encyclopedia of Science,* Second Edition.

Suggestions

We welcome any comments on this work and suggestions for entries to feature in future editions of *U•X•L Encyclopedia of Science*. Please write: Editors, *U•X•L Encyclopedia of Science,* U•X•L, Gale Group, 27500 Drake Road, Farmington Hills, Michigan, 48331-3535; call toll-free: 800-877-4253; fax to: 248-699-8097; or send an e-mail via www.galegroup.com.

Entries by Scientific Field

Biology

Electrical engineering

Electronics

Entries by
Scientific Field

P

Paleoecology

Paleoecology is the study of fossil organisms and their relationship to ancient environments. Paleoecology falls under the broader category of paleontology (the study of fossils). A person who studies and investigates paleoecology is called a paleoecologist. The study of paleoecology is important to scientists because it reveals so much about such natural aspects of ancient history as wind conditions, climates, temperatures, and ocean activity. Critical to the field of paleoecology is the intense concentration of chemicals found in fossils; such chemical data reveals much information about the world of long, long ago.

The field of paleoecology was developed by American geologist (a person who studies the history of Earth) Kirk Bryan (1888–1950). Bryan focused his investigations on weather changes from the past by using information from ancient soils and pollen. His work gathered enough interest from the scientific community to help develop the field of paleoecology.

Paleoecologists can find clues about the ancient environment and the organisms that lived during a particular time on Earth by examining fossil organisms, the different varieties of those fossils, and the sediment in which they were found. Sediment is made up of rock particles, minerals, and fossil organisms that, due to the forces of weather and time, have deposited on top of each other, forming layers. These layers compress and harden, forming sedimentary rock.

Sediment also collects at the bottom of an estuary (area of water where the sea meets a river). Each layer of sediment represents a piece of time in history. Paleoecologists take core samples of the sediment—

by pushing a tube down into the estuary and pulling out a sample of the muddy bottom—that provide a historical record of the past. Material found closest to the top of the tube is the youngest sediment; material near the bottom of the tube sample is the oldest. (The idea of sediment layers is similar to that of tree rings, which reveal the age of a tree.)

For example, marine (sea-dwelling) fossils have a significant accumulation of chemicals in their skeletons. By studying these chemicals, paleoecologists can draw conclusions about what was happening in the environment and what was living in the areas surrounding oceans. Be-

A Devonian plant fossil.
(Reproduced by permission of the Corbis Corporation [Bellevue].)

Words to Know

Fossils: The remains, traces, or impressions of living organisms that inhabited Earth more than ten thousand years ago.

Paleontology: The scientific study of the life of past geological periods as known from fossil remains.

Sediment: Sand, silt, clay, rock, gravel, mud, or other matter that has been transported by flowing water.

Sedimentary rock: Rock formed from compressed and solidified layers of organic or inorganic matter.

cause of what is recorded in fossils found in water environments, paleoecologists most frequently study these types of fossils.

[*See also* **Fossil and fossilization; Paleontology**]

Paleontology

Paleontology is the study of ancient life-forms of past geologic periods. Paleontologists learn about ancient animals and plants mainly through the study of fossils. These may be the actual remains of the animal or plant or simply traces the organism left behind (tracks, burrows, or imprints left in fine sediments).

Paleozoology is the subdiscipline of paleontology that focuses on the study of ancient animal life. Paleobotany is the subdiscipline that focuses on the study of the plant life of the geologic past.

Geologic time is a scale geologists have devised to divide Earth's 4.5-billion-year history into units of time. A unit is defined by the fossils or rock types found in it that makes it different from other units. The largest units are called eras. Periods are blocks of time within eras, while epochs are blocks of time within periods.

Scientists believe the earliest life-forms (primitive bacteria and algae) appeared on Earth some four billion years ago, at the beginning of the Precambrian era. Over time, these simple one-celled microorganisms evolved into soft-bodied animals and plants. To be preserved as a fossil,

Words to Know

Extinction: Condition in which all members of a group of organisms cease to exist.

Fossil: Remains of an ancient animal or plant, usually preserved in sedimentary rock.

Geologic time: Period of time covering the formation and development of Earth.

Invertebrate: Animal that lacks a backbone.

Vertebrate: Animal with a backbone.

an animal must have a hard shell or bony structure. For this reason, there are no fossils older than about 600 million years, which marks the beginning of the Paleozoic era.

Age of Invertebrates

Paleontologists label the beginning of the Paleozoic era as the Age of Invertebrates. Invertebrates are animals that lack a backbone (a spinal column encased in vertebrae). The first period of the Paleozoic era, the Cambrian period, saw an explosion of invertebrate evolution, giving rise to every group of invertebrates that have existed on Earth. The main or dominant invertebrates during the Cambrian period were trilobytes—flat, oval marine animals. All animals during the Cambrian period, which lasted until about 500 million years ago, lived in the oceans.

Age of Fishes

The fourth period of the Paleozoic era, lasting from 405 to 345 million years ago, is known as the Devonian period. This period saw the rise of fishes as the dominant life-form, and therefore marks the beginning of the Age of Fishes. The first vertebrates (animals with a backbone) were fishes, although these early fishes lacked jaws. The Devonian period also saw the rise of the earliest plants (such as ferns and mosses), insects, and amphibians (the first vertebrates to leave the oceans for dry land).

Age of Reptiles

Reptiles—cold-blooded, air-breathing vertebrates that lay eggs—first evolved from amphibians about 320 million years ago during the Carboniferous period (fifth period of the Paleozoic era). They became the dominant species on land, however, during the Permian period, the last period of the Paleozoic era. Hence, this period marks the beginning of what is known as the Age of Reptiles. Lasting from about 280 to 250 years ago, the Permian period also saw the mass extinction of over 90 percent of marine species.

Reptiles continued to dominate the planet during the next era, the Mesozoic era, which lasted from about 250 to 65 million years ago. This era also saw the rise of the earliest flying reptiles and birds, conifers (cone-bearing) and deciduous trees, and flowering plants and grasses. However, this era is most prominently marked by the evolution of smaller reptiles into the dinosaurs, who appeared about 225 million years ago during the Triassic period (first period of the Mesozoic era). Dinosaurs roamed and governed the world for about 160 million years before they were wiped out in a mass extinction 65 million years ago. Scientists believe a huge asteroid struck Earth off the northern tip of the Yucatan Peninsula of Mexico. The resulting inferno from the impact killed hundreds of thousands of species and brought an end to the reign of the dinosaurs.

Researchers cleaning dinosaur fossils in a paleontology laboratory in Esperanza, France. The fossils arrive encased in a protective plaster cast and with some of the surrounding rock still attatched. They are cleaned thoroughly and treated with stabilizing chemicals before being studied or classified. *(Reproduced by permission of Photo Researchers, Inc.)*

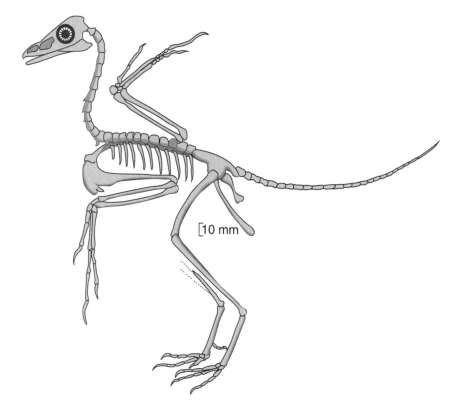

[10 mm

Paelontolgists use the bones they find to figure out the complete structure of different extinct animals. *(Reproduced by permission of The Gale Group.)*

Age of Mammals

The Cenozoic era, the last 65 million years of Earth's history, has seen the rise of warm-blooded mammals as the dominant form of life. Although the first land mammals were not as large as dinosaurs, they were much larger than present-day mammals. Around one million years ago, during the Pleistocene epoch of the Quaternary period, ancestors of modern humans became dominant, with many species of mammals becoming extinct in the process.

[*See also* **Dinosaur; Evolution; Fish; Fossil and fossilization; Geologic time; Human evolution; Invertebrates; Mammals; Paleoecology; Reptiles; Vertebrates**]

Paper

Paper is an indispensable part of everyday life. Beyond its use as the basic material for written and printed communication, paper in its various forms are used for hundreds of other purposes, including packaging, wrap-

▼ Words to Know

Calendar rolls: Highly polished metal rollers used to compact and smooth paper after it has dried.

Cellulose: An insoluble carbohydrate that plants use as building material to make their cell walls.

Deckle: Frame around the edges of a mold used to make paper by hand; also, either of the straps around the edge of the screening of a papermaking machine.

Fourdrinier machine: Machine that forms paper from pulp, named after the English brothers who financed its development in the early nineteenth century.

ping, insulating, and toweling. Each year, Americans use an average of 750 pounds (340 kilograms) of paper products per person. That equates to 210 billion pounds (95 billion kilograms) of paper products used in the United States per year.

The word paper comes from papyrus, a reedy plant that used to grow abundantly along the Nile River in Egypt. Centuries ago, ancient Egyptians removed the fibrous layers from the stem of this plant and cemented them together to create a durable woven writing material also known as papyrus. Examples of papyrus manuscripts have survived to the present.

Many sources claim that paper (as we know it) was first invented in A.D. 105 by Ts'ai Lun, a Chinese court official. Historians believe he mixed mulberry bark, hemp, and rags with water, mashed it into a pulp, pressed out the liquid, then hung the thin mat on a mold of bamboo strips to dry in the Sun. Paper made from rags in about A.D. 150 still exists today.

By the early seventh century, paper and its production had been introduced into Japan. From here, it spread to Central Asia by 750. Paper did not make its way into Europe until about 1150, but it spread throughout the continent over the next few centuries. Rags were the chief source of paper fibers until the introduction of papermaking machinery in the early nineteenth century, when it became possible to obtain papermaking fibers from wood.

Today, paper can be both handmade and machine-made. Both types of paper consist of tiny cellulose fibers pressed together in a thin sheet.

Each of these fibers is a tiny tube, about 100 times as long as it is wide. Today, most fibers come from wood, though in earlier times, the source was more likely to have been rags of linen or cotton. The source material is reduced to a slurry of fibers that float freely in water, and many of the fibers will have been broken or cut when making the pulp. When the water is removed, the fibers form a thin layer of pulp that eventually becomes paper.

Handmade paper

Rags to be made into paper are first sorted, and any unsuitable ones are discarded. Seams are opened and items such as buttons are removed. The rags are chopped into small pieces, which are then boiled in strong cleansing solutions. Next, the pieces are rinsed and beaten while damp until all of the threads have disintegrated and the fibers float freely in water. This is the paper pulp.

A French papermaker tearing cotton rags to incorporate into the paper mixture, to make fine, heavyweight paper. *(Reproduced by permission of the Corbis Corporation [Bellevue].)*

The very dilute pulp is next sent to the vat where the paper will actually be made. A rectangular mold containing wires running at right angles to each other is used to make a film of the pulp. Traditional molds have thin, closely spaced parallel wires running across the mold at the surface. These are attached to thick, widely spaced wires beneath them that run perpendicular or in the opposite direction. Paper formed on this type of mold typically reveals a ladder-like pattern when held up to the light, and is known as laid paper. Woven paper is formed on a mold of plain, woven wire screening. Thin wire forming a design may be attached to the mold's surface wires to produce a watermark in the finished paper. A rectangular frame, called the deckle, is placed over the mold to convert the mold into a sort of tray.

The papermaker then dips the mold with the deckle attached into the vat of dilute pulp and draws up a small amount of pulp on the surface of the wire. The mold is then shaken and tilted until most of the water has drained through the wire. The deckle is removed, and additional water is allowed to drain off. A second worker takes the mold and transfers the film of pulp to a piece of damp felt, laying a second piece of felt across the top.

This process continues until a stack of alternating wet paper and felt has built up. The stack is placed in a press to eliminate any residual

Old, used paper is easily recycled into new, reusable paper. *(Reproduced by permission of the Corbis Corporation [Bellevue].)*

water. Then the paper and felt are separated, and the paper is pressed by itself and hung up to dry. When dry, the paper sheets are dipped in a tub containing gelatin or very dilute glue and dried again. This gives the paper a harder and less absorbent finish than it would otherwise have had.

All paper was made by hand until the early nineteenth century. Artists use most of the handmade paper produced today, although many other people believe it to be the finest printing surface available.

Machine-made paper

Hardly any paper for book printing is made from rags today. Wood is the main ingredient of paper pulp, though the better papers contain cotton fiber, and the best are made entirely of cotton. The fibers are converted into pulp by chemical or mechanical means. Chemical pulp is used to make fine white paper, whereas mechanical pulp is used to make newsprint, tissue, towel, and other inexpensive papers.

Chemical pulp begins with the debarking of logs. Chippers with whirling blades reduce the logs to smaller and smaller chips. The wood chips are then boiled in a large vat called a digester that contains strong caustic solutions that dissolve away parts of the wood that are not cellulose. This leaves only pure fibers of cellulose.

Machinery at a papermill, spreading the paper pulp out over a grid to drain the water out of it. *(Reproduced by permission of the Corbis Corporation [Bellevue].)*

Mechanical pulp also begins with debarked logs. The logs are then ground up into fibers by a rapidly revolving grindstone. Spruce, balsam, and hemlock are the woods considered best suited for pulping by this process. Unlike chemical pulp, mechanical pulp contains all of the parts of the original wood. Because of this, mechanical pulp is weak and tends to discolor quickly. If mechanical pulp is to be used to make white paper, it is usually bleached with chlorine dioxide or sodium hydroxide. Paper pulp used to be bleached with chlorine, but the U.S. Environmental Protection Agency (EPA) determined that the process of bleaching paper with chlorine produces dioxin, a carcinogen or cancer-causing agent. In 1998, the EPA mandated that paper companies switch to safer compounds

The machine that converts either type of pulp into paper is called a fourdrinier machine, after English brothers Henry and Sealy Fourdrinier, who financed its development in 1803. The fourdrinier machine takes pulp that is almost 100 percent water and, by removing almost all the water, changes it into a continuous web of paper.

Watery pulp enters the fourdrinier machine on an endless moving belt of nylon mesh screening. As it moves forward, the screening is agitated from side to side to drain the excess water. Deckle straps prevent the liquid pulp from slopping over the sides. Air suction pumps beneath the screening also pull more water through. As the pulp passes along on the belt, a turning cylinder presses on it from above. This cylinder, called a dandy roll, is covered with wire mesh that imparts either a wove or a laid surface to pulp, depending on the pattern of the mesh.

At the end of the fourdrinier machine is a series of felt-covered rollers. As the pulp (now very wet paper) passes through them, they press still more water out of it, condensing the fibers. The paper then passes through sets of smooth metal press rollers that give a smooth finish to both surfaces of the paper. The drying process is completed after the fully formed paper passes through a series of large heated rollers. Once dried, the paper undergoes calendaring, in which it is pressed between a series of smooth metal (calendar) rollers that give it a polished surface. Afterward, the paper is cut into sheets or wrapped into a roll.

Parasites

A parasite is an organism that depends on another organism, known as a host, for food and shelter. As an example, tapeworms live in the digestive system of a large variety of animals. The tapeworms have no

Words to Know

Arthropod: A phylum of organisms characterized by exoskeletons and segmented bodies.

Definitive host: The organism in which a parasite reaches reproductive maturity.

Helminths: A variety of wormlike animals.

Intermediate host: An organism infected by a parasite while the parasite is in a developmental form, not sexually mature.

Nematodes: A type of helminth characterized by long, cylindrical bodies; commonly known as roundworms.

Protozoa: Single-celled animal-like microscopic organisms that must live in the presence of water.

Trematodes: A class of worms characterized by flat, oval-shaped bodies; commonly known as flukes.

Vector: Any agent, living or otherwise, that carries and transmits parasites and diseases.

digestive system of their own, but absorb nutrients through their skin from partially digested food as it passes through the host.

A parasite usually gains all the benefits of this relationship. In contrast, the host may suffer from various diseases, infections, and discomforts as a result of the parasitic attack. In some cases, however, the host may show no signs at all of infection by the parasite.

The life cycle of a typical parasite commonly includes several developmental stages. During these stages, the parasite may go through two or more changes in body structure as it lives and moves through the environment and one or more hosts.

Parasites that remain on a host's body surface to feed are called ectoparasites, while those that live inside a host's body are called endoparasites. Parasitism is a highly successful biological adaptation. More parasitic species are known than nonparasitic ones. Parasites affect just about every form of life, including nearly all animals, plants, and even bacteria.

The study of parasites

Parasitology is the study of parasites and their relationships with host organisms. Throughout history, people have coped with over 100 types of parasites affecting humans. Parasites have not, however, been systematically studied until the last few centuries. With his invention of the microscope in the late 1600s, the Dutch scientist Anton von Leeuwenhoek (1632–1723) was perhaps the first person to observe microscopic parasites. As Westerners began to travel and work more often in tropical parts of the world, medical researchers had to study and treat a variety of new infections, many of which were caused by parasites. By the early 1900s, parasitology had developed as a specialized field of study.

Typically, a parasitic infection does not directly kill a host. The stress placed on the organism's resources can affect its growth, ability to reproduce, and survival. This stress can sometimes lead to the host's premature death. Parasites, and the diseases they cause and transmit, have been responsible for tremendous human suffering and loss of life throughout history. The majority of parasitic infections occur within tropical regions and among low-income populations. However, almost all regions of the world sustain parasitic species, and all humans are susceptible to infection.

Infectious diseases

An infectious disease, or infection, is a condition that results when a parasitic organism attacks a host and begins to multiply. As the parasite multiplies, it interferes with the normal life functions of the host more and more. The host begins to feel ill as a symptom of the parasite's invasion and activities. In many cases, the host's immune system (which fights foreign bodies in the body) may be able to respond to the parasite and destroy it. In many other cases, however, the parasitic infection may overwhelm the immune system, resulting in serious disease and even death.

Until a century ago, infections were the primary means of human "population control" worldwide, often killing enormous numbers of people in epidemics of diseases such as bubonic plague and typhoid fever. Even today, infections actually cause more deaths during war and famine than do actual injuries and starvation. Fortunately, many infectious diseases can now be treated by means of antibiotics and other drugs and by a variety of preventative methods.

Almost all infections contracted by humans pass from other humans or animals. Some infections originate from outside the body, among them a cold from kissing someone with a cold; rabies from a dog bite; hepatitis B from a contaminated needle entering the bloodstream; hepatitis A from germs transferred from fingers to mouth after touching a dirty toilet seat; measles, mumps, and the flu from tiny moisture particles that exit the mouth and nose when a person sneezes, coughs, or talks; syphilis from an infected sex partner; tetanus from a soil-contaminated wound; salmonella from ingesting undercooked eggs, meat, and poultry; and many diseases ranging from the relatively innocent to the fatal—such as gastroenteritis, cholera, and dysentery—from drinking or bathing in contaminated water.

Endogenous (caused by factors within the organism) infections occur when the host's resistance is lowered, perhaps by malnutrition, illness, trauma, or immune depression. Weakening of the host's immune system may permit normally harmless organisms already present in or on the host or in the environment to cause illness.

Types of parasites

The major types of organisms that cause parasitic infections include species of protozoa, helminths or worms, and arthropods.

Protozoa. Protozoa are single-celled organisms that carry out most of the same physiological functions as more complex organisms. More than 45,000 species of protozoa are known, many of which are parasitic. As parasites of humans, this group of organisms has historically been the cause of more suffering and death than any other category of disease-causing organisms.

Intestinal protozoa occur throughout the world. They are especially common in areas where food and water sources are subject to contamination from animal and human waste. Typically, protozoa that infect their host through water or food do so while in an inactive state, called a cyst. A cyst consists of a protozoan encased in a protective outer membrane. The membrane protects the organism as it travels through the digestive tract of a previous host. Once inside a new host, the parasite develops into a mature form that feeds and reproduces.

Amebic dysentery is one of the most common parasitic diseases. It often afflicts travelers who visit tropical and subtropical regions. The condition is characterized by diarrhea, vomiting and weakness. It is caused by a protozoan known as *Entamoeba histolytica.*

Another protozoan that causes severe diarrhea is *Giardia lamblia.* This organism was originally discovered by Leeuwenhoek and has been well-publicized as a parasite that can infect hikers who drink untreated water.

Other types of parasitic protozoa infect the blood or tissues of their hosts. These protozoa are typically transmitted through another organism, called a vector. A vector is an organism that carries a parasite from one host to another host. In many cases, the vector is an invertebrate, such as an insect that itself feeds on a host and then passes the protozoan on through the bite wound. Some of the most infamous of these protozoa are the ones that cause malaria and African sleeping sickness.

Helminths.   Helminths are wormlike organisms including nematodes (roundworms), cestodes (tapeworms), and trematodes (flukes). Leeches are also helminths and are considered ectoparasitic, since they attach themselves to the outside skin of their hosts.

One of the most infamous nematodes is *Trichinella spiralis.* At one stage of its life cycle, this nematode lives in the muscle tissue of animals, including swine. Eventually, these organisms make their way into the intestinal tissue of humans who happen to ingest infected, undercooked pork.

The largest parasitic roundworm, common among humans living in tropical developing countries, is *Ascaris lumbricoides.* This roundworm can grow to a length of 35 centimeters (15 inches) within the small intestine of its host.

A parasitic roundworm that affects dogs is *Dirofilaria immitus,* or heartworm. This worm infects the heart tissues and eventually weakens

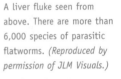

A liver fluke seen from above. There are more than 6,000 species of parasitic flatworms. *(Reproduced by permission of JLM Visuals.)*

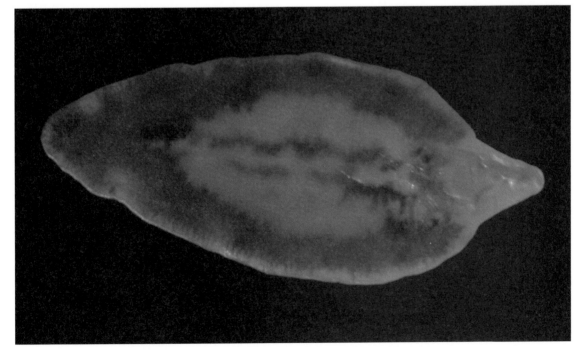

the cardiac (heart) muscles to the point of failure. If left untreated, heartworm can kill a dog.

Tapeworms are a class of worms characterized by their flat, segmented bodies. The segments hold both male and female reproductive organs, allowing self-fertilization. Segments that contain fertilized eggs break off or dissolve, passing the eggs out of the host. Adult tapeworms typically reside in the intestinal tract of vertebrates, attaching themselves to the stomach lining with hooks or suckers on their head.

Common tapeworms that attack humans are *Taenia saginata, Taenia solium,* and *Diphyllobothrium latum.* These parasites use intermediate hosts, such as cattle, swine, and fish respectively, before entering the human body. Parasites such as these infect an intermediate host organism while in a early developmental form. But they do not grow to maturity until they have been transmitted to the final host.

In the case of *Taenia* species, for example, tapeworm eggs are passed into cattle or swine through infected soil. They develop into an intermedi-

Entwined pair of male and female schistosomes. Adult pairs live in the small veins of human hosts, where the female produces about 3,500 eggs per day. *(Reproduced by permission of Phototake.)*

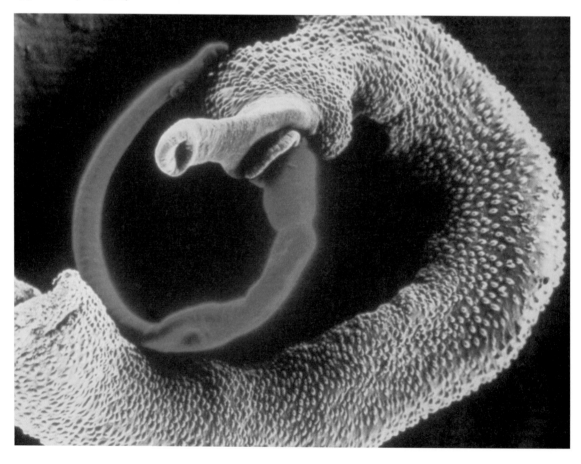

ary stage that embeds in the muscle and connective tissue of the animal. Infected animals that are processed for meat but improperly cooked still harbor the parasite, which are passed on when consumed by humans. The tapeworms develop into adults that attach to the intestinal lining of the host.

Trematodes, or flukes, are another class of helminths that have parasitic species. Adult flukes are typically flat, oval-shaped worms that have a layer of muscles just below the skin. These muscles allow the worm to expand and contract its shape and, thus, move its body. Flukes usually have an oral sucker, sometimes ringed with hooks. They use the sucker to attach themselves to the host's tissues.

Some of the most infamous flukes are species of the genus *Schistosoma* that cause the often-fatal disease known as schistosomiasis. These flukes infect human hosts directly by burrowing into the skin of a person wading or swimming in infected water. One species, *S. mansoni,* enters the bloodstream as an immature worm and can be carried through various organs, including the lungs and heart, before maturing in the liver.

Arthropods. Arthropods are organisms characterized by exterior skeletons and segmented bodies. Examples include the crustaceans, insects, and arachnids. The arthropods are the most diverse and widely distributed animals on the planet. Many arthropod species serve as carriers of bacterial and viral diseases, as intermediate hosts for protozoan and helminth parasites, and as parasites themselves.

Certain insect species are the carriers of some of humanity's most dreaded diseases, including malaria, typhus, and plague. As consumers of agricultural crops and parasites of our livestock, insects are also humankind's number-one competitor for resources.

Mosquitoes are the most notorious carriers of disease and parasites. Female mosquitoes rely on warm-blooded hosts to serve as a blood meal to nourish their eggs. During the process of penetrating a host's skin with their long, sucking mouth parts, saliva from the mosquito is transferred into the bite area. Any viral, protozoan, or helminth infections carried in the biting mosquito can be transferred directly into the blood stream of its host. Among these diseases are malaria, yellow fever, filariasis, elephantiasis, and heartworm.

Flies also harbor diseases that can be transmitted to humans and other mammals when they bite to obtain a blood meal for themselves. For example, black flies can carry Onchocerciasis (which causes river blindness), sandflies can carry leishmaniasis and kala-azar, and tsetse flies can carry the trypanosomes that cause sleeping sickness. Livestock, such as horses and cattle, can be infected with a variety of botflies and warbles that infest and feed on the skin, throat, nasal passages, and stomachs of their hosts.

Fleas and lice are two of the most common and irritating parasitic insects of humans and livestock. Lice commonly live among the hairs of their hosts, feeding on blood. Some species are carriers of typhus fever. Fleas usually infest birds and mammals, and can feed on humans when they are transferred from pets or livestock. Fleas are known to carry a variety of devastating diseases, including the plague.

Another prominent class of arthropods that contains parasitic species is the arachnids. Included in this group are spiders, scorpions, ticks, and mites.

Mites are very small arachnids that infest both plants and animals. One common type of mite is the chigger, which lives in grasses. As larvae, they may grab onto passing animals and attach themselves to the skin, often leading to irritating rashes or bite wounds. Scabies are another

A photo of a flea magnified 50 times. Fleas are common parasitic insects that are known to carry a variety of devastating diseases, including the plague. *(Reproduced by permission of The Stock Market.)*

mite that causes mange in some mammals by burrowing into the skin and producing severe scabs, lesions, and loss of hair.

Ticks also live their adult lives among grasses and short shrubs. They are typically larger than mites. The adult female tick attaches itself to an animal host for a blood meal. Tick bites themselves can be painful and irritating. More importantly, ticks can carry a number of diseases that affect humans. The most common of these diseases include Rocky Mountain spotted fever, Colorado tick fever, and Lyme disease.

Control of parasites

Many parasitic infections can be treated by a variety of medical procedures, such as the use of antibiotics. The best way of controlling infection, however, is prevention. Scientists have developed and continue to test a number of drugs that can be taken as a barrier to certain parasites. Other measures of control include improving sanitary conditions of water and food sources, proper cooking techniques, education about personal hygiene, and control of intermediate and vector host organisms.

[*See also* **Arachnids; Arthropods; Plague; Protozoa**]

Particle accelerators

Particle accelerators (also known as atom-smashers) are devices used for increasing the velocity of subatomic particles such as protons, electrons, and positrons. Although they were originally invented for the purpose of studying the basic structure of matter, particle accelerators later found a number of practical applications.

There are two large subgroups of particle accelerators: linear and circular accelerators. Machines of the first type accelerate particles as they travel in a straight line, sometimes over very great distances. Circular accelerators move particles along a circular or spiral path in machines that vary in size from less than a few feet to many miles in diameter.

The Van de Graaff accelerator

One of the earliest particle accelerators developed was invented by Alabama-born physicist Robert Jemison Van de Graaff (1901–1967) in about 1929. The machine that now bears his name illustrates the fundamental principles on which all particle accelerators are based.

▼ Words to Know

Cyclotron: A particle accelerator in which subatomic particles are accelerated to high speeds in a circular path.

Dee: An electrically charged metallic container that makes up half of a cyclotron. Particles pass from one dee to another as they travel back and forth through the machine.

Drift tube: A cylindrical tube in a linear accelerator through which particles are accelerated.

Electron: A fundamental particle of matter carrying a single unit of negative electrical charge.

Electron volt (eV): A unit used to measure the energy of subatomic particles in a particle accelerator.

Linear accelerator: A particle accelerator in which subatomic particles are accelerated to high speeds in a straight line.

Potential difference: Also called voltage; the amount of electric energy stored in a mass of electric charges compared to the energy stored in some other mass of charges.

Proton: A fundamental particle of matter carrying a single unit of positive electrical charge.

Radiation: Energy transmitted in the form of electromagnetic waves or subatomic particles.

Subatomic particle: Basic unit of matter and energy smaller than an atom.

Superconducting Supercollider: A particle accelerator designed to be the most powerful machine of its kind in the world.

Synchrotron radiation: A form of radiation (energy in the form of waves or particles) somewhat similar to X rays given off by certain kinds of particle accelerators.

Velocity: The rate at which the position of an object changes with time, including both the speed and the direction.

The Van de Graaff accelerator consists of a tall metal cylinder with a hollow metal dome at its top. A silk conveyor belt runs through the middle of the cylinder. At the bottom of the cylinder, the belt collects positive charges from a high-voltage source. The positive charges ride to the top of the cylinder on the belt and are deposited on the outside of the dome at the top of the machine. The longer the belt runs, the more positive charges accumulate on the dome. The original Van de Graaff accelerator could produce an accumulation of charge with an energy of 80,000 volts, although later improvements raised that value to 5,000,000 volts.

At some point, the accumulation of charges on the hollow dome becomes so great that a bolt of lightning jumps from the dome to a metal rod near the machine. The bolt of lightning consists of positive charges that accumulate on the dome and are finally repelled from it.

The Van de Graaff accelerator can be converted to a particle accelerator simply by attaching some kind of target to the metal rod near the machine. When the bolt of lightning strikes the metal rod, it will bombard the target. Atoms of which the target is made will be broken apart by the beam of positively charged electricity.

Linear accelerators

In a Van de Graaff generator, the bolt of lightning that travels from the dome to the target consists of charged particles whose velocity has increased from zero (while at rest on the dome) to more than 100,000 miles per second (160,000 kilometers per second) in the gap between dome and target. Linear accelerators (also known as linacs) operate on the same general principle, except that a particle is exposed to a series of electrical fields, each of which increases the velocity of the particle.

A typical linac consists of a few hundred or a few thousand cylindrical metal tubes arranged one in front of another. The tubes are electrically charged so that each carries a charge opposite that of the tube on either side of it. Tubes 1, 3, 5, 7, 9, etc., might, for example, be charged positively, and tubes 2, 4, 6, 7, 10, etc., charged negatively.

Imagine that a negatively charged electron is introduced into a linac just in front of the first tube. In the circumstances described above, the electron is attracted by and accelerated toward the first tube. The electron passes toward and then into that tube. Once inside the tube, the electron no longer feels any force of attraction or repulsion and merely drifts through the tube until it reaches the opposite end. It is because of this behavior that the cylindrical tubes in a linac are generally referred to as drift tubes.

At the moment that the electron leaves the first drift tube, the charge on all drift tubes is reversed. Tubes 1, 3, 5, 7, 9, etc. are now negatively charged, and tubes 2, 4, 6, 8, 10, etc. are positively charged. The electron exiting the first tube now finds itself repelled by the tube it has just left and attracted to the second tube. These forces of attraction and repulsion provide a kind of "kick" that accelerates the electron in a forward direction. It passes through the space between tubes 1 and 2 and into tube 2. Once again, the electron drifts through this tube until it exits at the opposite end.

As the electron moves through the linac, the electric charge on all drift tubes reverses in a regular pattern. As it passes through the tube, the electron is repelled by the tube behind it and attracted to the tube ahead of it. The added energy it receives is exhibited in a greater velocity. As a result, the electron is moving faster in each new tube it enters and can cover a greater distance in the same amount of time. To make sure that the electron exits a tube at just the right moment, the tubes must be of different lengths. Each one is slightly longer than the one before it.

The largest linac in the world is the Stanford Linear Accelerator, located at the Stanford Linear Accelerator Center (SLAC) in Stanford, California. An underground tunnel 3 kilometers (2 miles) in length passes beneath U.S. Highway 101 and holds 82,650 drift tubes along with the magnetic, electrical, and auxiliary equipment needed for the machine's operation. Electrons accelerated in the SLAC linac leave the end of the machine traveling at nearly the speed of light with a maximum energy of about 32 GeV (gigaelectron volts).

The Vivitron electrostatic particle accelerator at the Centre des Recherches Nucléaires in Strasbourg, France. Vivitron, the largest Van de Graaff generator in the world, can generate a potential of up to 35 million volts. The accelerator is used to fire ions of elements such as carbon at other nuclei. Gamma rays given off by these nuclei reveal much about the internal structure of the nucleus. *(Reproduced by permission of Photo Researchers, Inc.)*

The term electron volt (eV) is the standard unit of energy measurement in accelerators. It is defined as the energy lost or gained by an electron as it passes through a potential difference of one volt. Most accelerators operate in the megaelectron volt (million electron volt; MeV), gigaelectron volt (billion electron volt; GeV), or teraelectron volt (trillion electron volt; TeV) range.

Circular accelerators

The development of linear accelerators is limited by some obvious physical constraints. For example, the SLAC linac is so long that engineers had to take into consideration Earth's curvature when they laid out the drift tube sequence. One way of avoiding the problems associated with the construction of a linac is to accelerate particles in a circle. Machines that operate on this principle are known, in general, as circular accelerators.

The earliest circular accelerator, the cyclotron, was invented by University of California professor of physics Ernest Orlando Lawrence (1901–1958) in the early 1930s. Lawrence's cyclotron added to the design of the linac one new fundamental principle from physics: a charged particle that passes through a magnetic field travels in a curved path. The shape of the curved path depends on the velocity of the particle and the strength of the magnetic field.

The cyclotron consists of two hollow metal containers that look as if a tuna fish can had been cut in half vertically. Each half resembles an uppercase letter D, so the two parts of the cyclotron are known as dees. At any one time, one dee in the cyclotron is charged positively and the other negatively. The dees are connected to a source of alternating current so that the electric charge on both dees changes back and forth many times per second.

The second major component of a cyclotron is a large magnet situated above and below the dees. The presence of the magnet means that any charged particles moving within the dees will travel not in straight paths but in curves.

Imagine that an electron (carrying a negative charge) is introduced into the narrow space between the two dees. The electron is accelerated into one of the dees, the one carrying a positive charge. As it moves, however, the electron travels toward the dee in a curved path.

After a fraction of a second, the current in the dees changes signs. The electron is then repelled by the dee toward which it first moved, reverses direction, and heads toward the opposite dee with an increased velocity. Again, the electron's return path is curved because of the magnetic field surrounding the dees.

Just as a particle in a linac passes through one drift tube after another, always gaining energy, so does a particle in a cyclotron travel back and forth between dees gaining energy. As the particle gains energy, it picks up speed and spirals outward from the center of the machine. Eventually, the particle reaches the outer circumference of the machine, passes out through a window, and strikes a target.

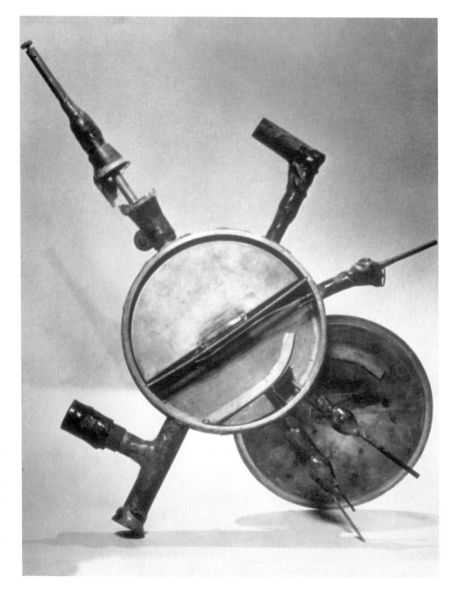

The first successful cyclotron, built in 1930 by Ernest Lawrence at the University of California at Berkeley. Only 4.5 inches (12 centimeters) in diameter, it accelerated protons to 80,000 volts. *(Reproduced by permission of Photo Researchers, Inc.)*

Lawrence's original cyclotron was a modest piece of equipment, only 11 centimeters (4.5 inches) in diameter, capable of accelerating protons to an energy of 80,000 electron volts (80 keV). It was assembled from coffee cans, sealing wax, and leftover laboratory equipment. The largest accelerators of this design ever built were the 218-centimeter (86-inch) and 225-centimeter (87-inch) cyclotrons at the Oak Ridge National Laboratory and the Nobel Institute in Stockholm, Sweden, respectively.

Cyclotron modifications

At first, improvements in cyclotron design were directed at the construction of larger machines that could accelerate particles to greater velocities. Soon, however, a new problem arose. Physical laws state that nothing can travel faster than the speed of light. Thus, adding more and more energy to a particle will not make that particle's speed increase indefinitely. Instead, as the particle's velocity approaches the speed of light, additional energy supplied to it appears in the form of increased mass. A particle whose mass is constantly increasing, however, begins to travel in a path different from that of a particle with constant mass. There is a practical significance to this fact: as the velocity of particles in a cyclotron begins to approach the speed of light, those particles start to fall "out of synch" with the current change that drives them back and forth between dees.

Two different modifications—or a combination of the two—can be made in the basic cyclotron design to deal with this problem. One approach is to gradually change the rate at which the electrical field alternates between the dees. The goal here is to have the sign change occur at the exact moment that particles have reached a certain point within the dees. As the particles speed up and gain weight, the rate at which electrical current alternates between the two dees slows down to "catch up" with the particles.

In the 1950s, a number of machines containing this design element were built in various countries. Those machines were known as frequency modulated (FM) cyclotrons, synchrocyclotrons, or, in the former Soviet Union, phasotrons. The maximum particle energy attained with machines of this design ranged from about 100 MeV to about 1 GeV.

A second solution for the mass increase problem is to alter the magnetic field of the machine in such a way as to maintain precise control over the particles' paths. This principle has been incorporated into the synchrotrons—machines that are now the most powerful cyclotrons in the world.

A synchrotron consists essentially of a hollow circular tube (the ring) through which particles are accelerated. (The particles are actually accelerated to velocities close to the speed of light in smaller machines before they are injected into the main ring.) Once they are within the main ring, particles receive additional jolts of energy from accelerating chambers placed at various locations around the ring. At other locations around the ring, very strong magnets control the path followed by the particles. As particles pick up energy and tend to spiral outward, the magnetic fields are increased, pushing particles back into a circular path. The most powerful synchrotrons now in operation can produce particles with energies of at least 400 GeV.

In the 1970s, nuclear physicists proposed the design and construction of the most powerful synchrotron of all, the Superconducting Super Collider (SSC). The SSC was expected to have an accelerating ring 82.9 kilometers (51.5 miles) in circumference with the ability to produce particles having an energy of 20 TeV. Estimated cost of the SSC was originally set at about $4 billion. Shortly after construction of the machine at Waxahachie, Texas, began, however, the U.S. Congress decided to discontinue funding for the project.

Applications

By far the most common use of particle accelerators is for basic research on the composition of matter. The quantities of energy released in such machines are unmatched anywhere on Earth. At these energy levels, new forms of matter are produced that do not exist under ordinary conditions. These forms of matter provide clues about the ultimate structure of matter.

Accelerators have also found some important applications in medical and industrial settings. As particles travel through an accelerator, they give off a form of radiation known as synchrotron radiation. This form of radiation is somewhat similar to X rays and has been used for similar purposes.

[*See also* **Subatomic particles**]

Perception

Perception is the quality of being aware of the conditions in one's environment. For example, visual perception refers to the ability of an organism to see objects in the world around it. Other forms of perception involve the senses of touch, smell, taste, and sound.

Perception is not a passive activity. That is, one way to think of visual perception is to say that light rays bounce off an object an enter one's eyes. Those light rays then create a "sight" message that travels to the person's brain where the object is recorded. But that explanation is incomplete. The brain also acts on the message received from the eyes in ways that are not totally understood by scientists. The important point is that the real world is not necessarily the world that one perceives.

A classic experiment illustrates this point. A group of young boys are all asked to look carefully at a nickel. The nickel is then taken away, and the boys are asked to draw a picture of the nickel. Boys in this experiment who come from wealthy families tend to draw the nickel smaller in size than boys from poor families. Each boy's perception of the nickel is affected to some extent by how important a nickel is in his life.

The biology of perception

All systems of perception have a common structure. They consist of cells designed specifically to detect some aspect of the surrounding environment, a series of neurons (nerve cells) that transmit the perceived information to the brain, and a specific segment of the brain for receiving and analyzing that information.

Depth perception—especially how the mind sees in three dimensions though the retina on which the image is registered as flat—continues to puzzle scientists. *(Reproduced by permission of Field Mark Publications.)*

Receptor cells can be classified according to the kind of stimuli to which they respond. Chemoreceptors, for example, are cells that detect certain kinds of chemical substances. Receptor cells in the nose and mouth are examples of chemoreceptors. Photoreceptors are another kind of receptor cell. Photoreceptors detect the presence of light. Mechanoreceptors detect changes in mechanical energy, changes that occur during touch and hearing and in maintaining the body's equilibrium (balance).

Messages received by any kind of receptor cell are passed through a network of neurons into the spine and on to the brain. There, messages are received and analyzed. Visual messages are analyzed in the visual cortex, for example, and messages from the ears in the auditory cortex.

Puzzling questions

Even with our fairly complete understanding of the biology of perception, some intriguing questions remain. Those questions cannot, as yet, be answered strictly in terms of the physical make-up of an organism's body. One of these questions has to deal with constancy. The term constancy refers to the fact that our perception of objects tends to remain the same despite real changes that occur in their image on the retina of the eye.

For example, suppose that you walk down a street looking at the tallest building on the street. As you approach the building, its image on the retina of your eye gets larger and larger. Certain proportions of the building change also. Yet, your brain does not interpret these changes as real changes in the building itself. It continues to "see" the building as the same size and shape no matter how close or how far you are from it.

Another perception puzzle involves the perception of motion. The mystery lies in how perceived movement cannot be accounted for by the movement of an object's image across the retina. If that were so, movement of the observer, or even eye movement, would lead to perceived object movement. For example, when riding a bike, the rest of the world would be perceived as moving.

Depth perception.   One of the puzzles that has interested scientists for centuries is depth perception. Depth perception refers to the fact that our eyes see the world in three dimensions, the way it is actually laid out. The problem is that images that enter the eye strike the retina, an essentially flat surface, at the back of the eye. How can a flat image on the retina be "read" by the brain as a three-dimensional image?

An important element in the answer to this puzzle appears to be binocular vision. The term binocular vision refers to the fact that humans and most other organisms detect visual signals with two eyes. The two eyes, set slightly apart from each other, receive two slightly different images of the environment. By methods that are still not entirely understood, the brain is able to combine those two images to produce a binocular version of an image, a three-dimensional view of the environment.

[*See also* **Ear; Eye; Smell; Taste; Touch**]

Periodic function

A periodic function is an event that occurs repeatedly in a very regular manner. Suppose that you stand on the beach near a lighthouse. As you watch, the lighthouse's beam will sweep across the landscape in a very regular pattern. You might see the beam pointing directly at you every second, or every two seconds, or at some other regular interval. The

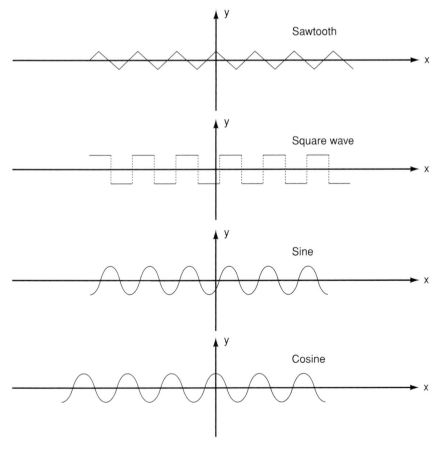

Figure 1. *(Reproduced by permission of The Gale Group.)*

regularity of a lighthouse beam is one of the ways in which ships at sea recognize the lighthouse and know where they are.

The graphical representation of a periodic function has a very characteristic shape. Figure 1 shows the most common of these shapes. In this graph, the vertical (y) axis shows the amplitude (magnitude) while the horizontal (x) axis shows time. As you go from left to right along the graph, it is as if you were moving forward in time. The origin (the point at which the two axes cross) represents zero time, and each additional second or minute or hour is represented by one unit to the right on the graph.

In the graph of the cosine, the amplitude at time zero is the highest it ever gets. If this graph represented the sweep of a lighthouse light, for example, point zero might be the time at which the light beam was pointing directly at you. As time passes (moving to the right on the x-axis), the amount of light you see (the amplitude) gradually decreases. Eventually it reaches its lowest possible point (the bottom of the curve). At that point, the light would be pointing directly away from you. Then, the light would continue its sweep until it was once more facing toward you.

One of the most important applications of periodic functions is in the study of electromagnetic radiation. Such diverse forms of energy as cosmic rays, X rays, ultraviolet light, infrared radiation, visible light, radar, radio waves, and microwaves all have one property in common: they are all periodic functions. Their properties and behavior can be studied by drawing graphical representations.

Periodic table

The periodic table is a chart that shows the chemical elements and their relationship to each other. The periodic table is a graphic way of representing the periodic law.

History of the periodic law

By the middle of the nineteenth century, about 50 chemical elements were known. One of the questions chemists were asking about those elements was the following: Is every element entirely different from every other element? Or are some elements related to other elements in some way? Are there patterns among the elements?

A number of chemists suggested various patterns. German chemist Johann Wolfgang Döbereiner (1780–1849) observed in 1829, for exam-

Words to Know

Atomic number: The number of protons in the nucleus of an atom; the number that appears over the element symbol in the periodic table.

Atomic weight: The average weight of all isotopes of a given element, expressed in units known as atomic mass units (amu).

Element: A pure substance that cannot be changed chemically into a simpler substance.

Family: A group of elements in the same column of the periodic table or in closely related columns of the table. (See Group.)

Group: A vertical column of the periodic table that contains elements possessing similar chemical characteristics. (See Family.)

Isotopes: Two or more forms of the same element with the same number of protons but different numbers of neutrons in the atomic nucleus.

Nucleus: The small core at the center of an atom that contains protons and (usually) neutrons.

Period: A horizontal row of elements in the periodic table. (See Row.)

Row: A horizontal set of elements in the periodic table. (See Period.)

ple, that three of the so-called halogen elements (chlorine, bromine, and iodine) could be classified according to their atomic weights. The atomic weight of bromine (79.9) turned out to be almost the exact average of the atomic weights of chlorine (35.5) and iodine (127), with $35.5 + 127 \div 2 = 81.25$ (almost 79.9)

Most of these classification schemes were not very successful. Then, in about 1869, two chemists made almost the same discovery at almost the same time. Russian chemist Dmitry Mendeleev (1834–1907) and German chemist Julius Lothar Meyer (1830–1895) suggested arranging the elements according to their atomic weights. In doing so, Mendeleev and Meyer pointed out, the properties of the elements appear to recur in a regular pattern.

Today, Mendeleev is usually given credit for discovering the periodic law because he took one step that Meyer did not. When all the elements are laid out in a table, some gaps appear. The reason for those gaps, Mendeleev said, was that other elements belonged there. But those elements had not yet been discovered.

Mendeleev went even further. He predicted the properties of those yet-to-be-discovered elements. He knew where they belonged in the periodic table, so he knew what elements they would be like. Remarkably, three of the elements Mendeleev predicted were discovered less than a decade after the periodic law was announced.

The modern periodic table

The periodic table used today is shown in Figure 1. It contains all of the known elements from the lightest (hydrogen: H) to the heaviest (meitnerium: Mt). Currently, there are 114 known elements, ranging from hydrogen, whose atoms have only one electron, to the as-yet unnamed element whose atoms contain 114 electrons. Each element has its own box in the periodic table. As shown in the sample at the top of the table, that box usually contains four pieces of information: the element's name, its symbol, its atomic number, and its atomic weight.

The table is divided in two directions, by rows and by columns. There are seven rows, called periods, and 18 columns, called groups or families. Two different numbering systems are used for the groups, as shown at the top of the table. The system using Roman numerals (IA, IIA, IIB, IVB, etc.) has traditionally been popular in the United States. The other system (1, 2, 3, 4, etc.) has traditionally been used in Europe and, a few years ago, was recommended for use in the United States as well.

Chemical elements in the same group tend to have similar chemical properties. Those in the same row have properties that change slowly from one end of the row to the other end. Figure 2 shows how one property—atomic radius—changes for certain elements in the table.

The appearance of the periodic table in Figure 1 is a little bit misleading, as is the case in almost every periodic table that is published. The reason for this misrepresentation is that two groups of elements shown at the bottom of the table actually belong within it. The Lanthanides, for example, belong in row 6 between lanthanum (#57) and hafnium (#72). Also, the Actinides belong in row 7 between actinium (#89) and unnilquadium (#104). The reason you don't see them there is that they simply don't fit. If they were actually inserted where they belong, the table would be much too wide to fit on a piece of paper or a wall chart. Thus, they are listed at the bottom of the table.

The diagonal line at the right of the table separates the elements into two major groups, the metals and nonmetals. Elements to the left of this line tend to be metals, while those to the right tend to be nonmetals. The elements that lie directly on the diagonal line are metalloids—elements that behave sometimes like metals and sometimes like nonmetals.

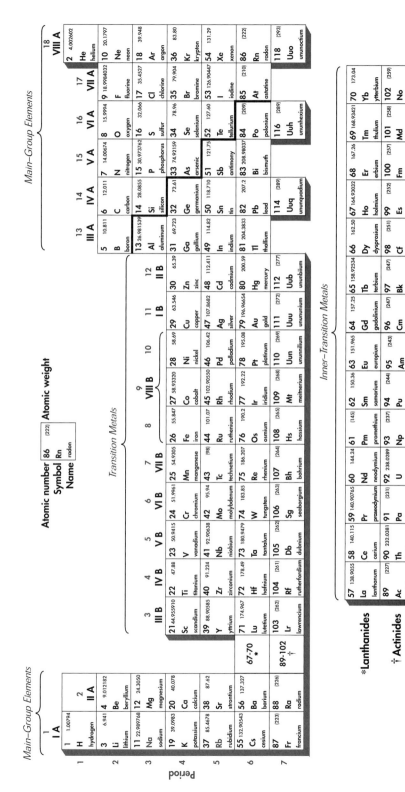

Figure 1. Periodic table of the elements. *(Reproduced by permission of The Gale Group.)*

The periodic table is one of the most powerful tools available to chemists and to chemistry students. Simply by knowing where an element is on the table, one can know a great deal about its physical and chemical properties.

Recent and future research

Recently, several man-made "superheavy" elements have been discovered. These include elements 110 and 111, both of which were made in late 1994 by an international team of scientists. Element 110 was made by colliding nickel atoms with an isotope of lead. Researchers in Russia have plans to make a different isotope of element 110 by colliding sulfur atoms with plutonium atoms. Elements 116 and 118 were recently discovered at a Berkeley, California, laboratory.

Other superheavy elements that have been predicted to exist have yet to be made in the laboratory, although research continues into the creation of these elements. Many exciting discoveries remain to be uncovered concerning the creation of new elements. With the periodic table as a guide, their place is already waiting for them.

[*See also* **Atom; Atomic mass; Element, chemical**]

Figure 2. Six representations of the atomic radii of the main-group elements. *(Reproduced by permission of The Gale Group.)*

	I A	II A	III A	IV A	V A	VIA	VIIA	VIIIA
Period 1	H							He
Period 2	Li	Be	B	C	N	O	F	Ne
Period 3	Na	Mg	Al	Si	P	S	Cl	Ar
Period 4	K	Ca	Ga	Ge	As	Se	Br	Kr
Period 5	Rb	Sr	In	Sn	Sb	Te	I	Xe
Period 6	Cs	Ba	Tl	Pb	Bi	Po	At	Rn

Petroglyphs and pictographs

Petroglyphs and pictographs are terms used by archaeologists to describe forms of rock carvings and paintings. Petroglyph refers to a rock carving or etching, while pictograph is commonly applied to a rock painting. Typically, these "rock art" examples are found in caves or under overhanging cliffs. Although both types of rock art can be traced back to early prehistoric times, many traditional aboriginal (native) cultures in Africa and Australia still practice the art of rock painting.

Origins of rock art

Some of the oldest known rock art features are pictographs. In France and Spain, cave paintings made by early humans have been dated to more than 30,000 years old. Located in deep, underground passages, they have been protected from rain, sunlight, and other ravages of time. Most of these colorful images are of animals such as deer, bison, and antelope. They are strikingly detailed and lifelike.

When humans migrated to North America some 12,000 years ago, they brought the practice of creating rock art with them. As time passed

Petroglyphs by an ancient American culture. *(Reproduced by permission of Field Mark Publications.)*

and people spread out across the Western Hemisphere, so did the use of rock art. Eventually, nearly all of the more than 200 distinct Native American tribes in North America used some form of rock art in their ceremonies. Interestingly, many of the artistic elements or patterns used in petroglyphs and pictographs are very similar among these diverse groups.

How rock art was created

From present-day cultures that continue to create rock art, archaeologists have learned that petroglyphs were made by using a handheld stone as a chisel or hammer to etch designs into boulders. Pictographs, however, were more complex to make because of the materials required for paint. Red pigments, which generally make up the most common color found in rock paintings, were made from iron oxides. Other minerals used to create colors were talc, gypsum, or lime for white; charcoal or graphite for black; and copper ores for greens and blues.

These minerals were ground into fine powders, then mixed with a resin, such as pine pitch. An oil base was sometimes added by grinding certain seeds or melting animal fat. Paints were applied either by fingers or with brushes made from animal fur, fibrous plant leaves, or the shredded end of a stick.

Rock art and the modern world

Many of the pictographs and petroglyphs created by ancient people have lasted for hundreds—even thousands—of years. However, modern pollutants and vandalism have recently hastened their destruction. Governments have passed laws protecting areas that contain such rock art. And scientists continue to study the chemical composition of these features, hoping one day to find an effective way to prevent further erosion and preserve these artistic works indefinitely.

Petroleum

Petroleum, also called crude oil, is a thick, flammable, yellow-to-black colored liquid. Petroleum was first found oozing out of rocks on Earth's surface. Hence, its name comes from the Latin words *petra,* meaning rock, and *oleum,* meaning oil. Petroleum is a hydrocarbon, an organic compound containing only carbon and hydrogen. It is a mixture of other hydrocarbon compounds such as natural gas, gasoline, kerosene, asphalt, and, probably most important, fuel oil.

Today, most scientists agree that oil was formed from the remains of plants and tiny animals that settled to the bottom of ancient oceans. These remains or sediments were buried by layers of mud and sand. Gradually, over millions of years, the weight of these accumulating layers built up great pressure and heat. The sediments packed together and became rock. The organic (once living) remains were changed into kerogen, a waxy substance that forms oil and natural gas. Most of the world's petroleum is more than 100 million years old, and is thus called a fossil fuel.

Unlike coal, which stays in one spot unless moved by Earth's shifting crust, oil slowly migrates upward through cracks and pores, or tiny holes, in nearby rocks. Eventually the oil reaches a solid layer of rock and becomes trapped underneath in a reservoir (pool). Natural gas often occurs in association with oil. Most of the world's petroleum reservoirs lie deep underground in structures called anticlines—gently folded layers of rock that form an arch above the deposit. Petroleum can also be trapped by fractured layers (or faults), salt formations, and stratigraphic (rock) traps. Some oil is also contained in shales (clay) and sands.

An oil-drilling rig in the southern United States. *(Reproduced by permission of Photo Researchers, Inc.)*

Location of world's supply

Although petroleum is found throughout the world, the Middle East possesses nearly two-thirds of all recoverable oil. Latin America contains about 13 percent, while the continents of Europe, North America, Asia, and Africa have only 4 to 8 percent each. Most North American oil is extracted in Alaska, Texas, California, Louisiana, and Oklahoma. The former Soviet republics, Saudi Arabia, and China are among the world's other leading oil producers. Their petroleum is sent to the United States for refining. While the United States possesses little of the world's petroleum supply (it must import more than 50 percent of its oil), it is one of the world's leading refiners. It is also the world's heaviest consumer of oil.

The importance of oil

Currently, petroleum is among our most important natural resources. We use gasoline, jet fuel, and diesel fuel to run cars, trucks, aircraft, ships, and other vehicles. Home heat sources include oil, natural gas, and electricity, which in many areas is generated by burning natural gas. Petroleum and petroleum-based chemicals are important in manufacturing plastic, wax, fertilizers, lubricants, and many other goods.

The 799-mile-long (1,286-kilometer-long) Trans-Alaska Pipeline is capable of transporting over 1.2 million barrels of oil per day. *(Reproduced by permission of JLM Visuals.)*

Different types of petroleum can be used in different ways. Refineries separate different petroleum products by heating petroleum to the point where heavy hydrocarbon molecules separate from lighter hydrocarbons. As a result, each product can be isolated and used for a specific purpose without waste. Thus, tar or asphalt, the dense, nearly solid hydrocarbons, can be used for road surfaces and roofing materials. Waxy substances called paraffins can be used to make candles and other similar products. And less dense, liquid hydrocarbons can be used for engine fuels.

The future of oil

The oil industry faces strong challenges. Environmental concerns are forcing companies to reevaluate all of their operations. Political unrest in the Middle East causes concern about access to oil supplies. And it is only a matter of time before oil supplies finally run out. According to some experts, that could be as soon as the mid-twenty-first century.

[*See also* **Fossil and fossilization; Internal-combustion engine; Natural gas; Oil drilling; Oil spills; Plastics; Pollution**]

pH

The most common method of indicating the acidity of a solution is by stating its pH. The term pH refers to a mathematical system developed by Danish chemist Søren Sørenson (1868–1939) around 1909. Sørenson originally suggested the term pH as an abbreviation for potential (or power) of hydrogen.

Acids and bases were first defined by Swedish chemist Svante Arrhenius (1859–1927). Arrhenius proposed that acids be defined as chemicals that produce positively charged hydrogen ions, H^+, in water. By comparison, he suggested that bases are compounds that produce negatively charged hydroxide ions, OH^-, in water.

The pH of a solution is determined by the concentration of hydrogen ions present—that is, by its acidity. The *more* hydrogen ions present (the more acidic the solution), the *lower* the pH. The *fewer* hydrogen ions present (the less acidic the solution), the *higher* the pH. The pH scale runs from 0 to 14. A pH value of 7 (in the middle of that range) represents a solution that is neither acidic nor basic.

Strong acids have very low pHs (battery acid has a pH of 0). Strong bases have very high pHs (sodium hydroxide, commonly known as lye,

Table 1.
Some Common Solutions and Their pH

Substance	Approximate pH
Battery acid (sulfuric acid)	0
Lemon juice	2
Vinegar	2.5
Coffee	5
Distilled water	7
Borax	9
Household ammonia solution	11
Lye (sodium hydroxide)	14

Table 2.
Some Common Indicators, the pH Range in Which They Change Color, and Their Color Changes

Indicator	pH Range	Color Changes
Methyl violet	pH 0.1 to 3.2	Yellow to violet
Bromophenol blue	pH 2.8 to 4.6	Yellow to blue–violet
Congo red	pH 3.0 to 5.0	Blue to red
Bromocresol purple	pH 5.2 to 6.8	Yellow to purple
Cresol red	pH 7.2 to 8.8	Yellow to purple
Phenolphthalein	pH 8.4 to 10.0	Colorless to pink
Brilliant orange	pH 10.5 to 12.0	Yellow to red
Titan yellow	pH 12.0 to 13.0	Yellow to red

has a pH of 14). Lemon juice has a pH of 2; vinegar of 2.5; coffee of 5; distilled water of 7; borax of 9; and household ammonia of 11.

pH indicators

One way of finding the pH of a solution is with a pH meter, a mechanical device that gives very precise readings. One can easily place the probe of a pH meter into a solution and read the pH of the solution on the meter dial.

A much older method for estimating the pH of a solution is the use of an indicator. A pH indicator is a material that changes color in solutions of different pH. One of the most common of all indicators is litmus.

Litmus is a chemical obtained from lichens. In the presence of a base, litmus is blue; in the presence of an acid, it is red.

Many indicators are extracted from plants. For example, you can make a reasonably good indicator just by boiling red cabbage and extracting the colored material produced. That material, like litmus, changes color in the presence of acids and bases. A number of indicators are synthetic products made just for testing the pH of solutions.

[*See also* **Acids and bases**]

Phobia

A phobia is an abnormal or irrational fear of a situation or thing. A person suffering from a phobia may dwell on the object of his or her fear when it is not even present. People have been known to have fears of things as common as running water, dirt, dogs, or high places. One in ten people develop a phobia at some time in their lives.

In addition to the emotional feeling of uncontrollable terror or dread, people suffering from a phobia (called phobics) may experience physical symptoms such as shortness of breath, trembling, rapid heartbeat, and an overwhelming urge to run. These symptoms are often so strong that they prevent phobic people from taking action to protect themselves.

Simple phobias are usually termed according to the specific object or situation feared. Examples include acrophobia (fear of heights), agoraphobia (open spaces), claustrophobia (enclosed spaces), mysophobia (dirt and germs), zoophobia (animals), arachnophobia (spiders), and ophediophobia (snakes).

Social phobias are triggered by social situations. Usually people with social phobias are afraid of being humiliated when they do something in front of others, such as speaking in public or even eating. People suffering from social phobias are often extremely shy.

Phobias can come about for a number of reasons. Psychologists believe that phobias begin when people have an extremely bad or negative experience with an object or situation. They then learn to equate those intense negative feelings with all future encounters with that same object or situation. Sometimes parents may pass irrational fears on to their children in this way.

One of the most effective treatments for phobias is a behavior therapy called exposure. The phobic is exposed to what is feared in the presence of the therapist and directly confronts the object or situation that causes terror. In addition to being treated with behavior therapy, phobics are sometimes given antianxiety drugs in order to lower their feelings of panic. Antidepressants are also used to control panic.

Photochemistry

Photochemistry is the study of chemical changes made possible by light energy. The production of ozone in Earth's upper atmosphere is an example of such a change. Light from the Sun (solar energy) strikes oxygen molecules in the stratosphere, causing them to break down into two oxygen atoms:

$$O_2 + h\nu \rightarrow O + O$$

(The expression $h\nu$ is commonly used to represent a unit of light energy known as the photon.)

In the next stage of that reaction, oxygen atoms react with oxygen molecules to produce ozone (O_3):

$$O + O_2 \rightarrow O_3$$

Steps in photochemical processes

The excited state.   A photochemical change takes place in two steps. Imagine that a light beam is shined on a piece of gold. The light beam can be thought of as a stream of photons, tiny packages of energy. The energy of the photon is expressed by means of the unit $h\nu$.

When a photon strikes an atom of gold, it may be absorbed by an electron in the gold atom. The electron then becomes excited, meaning that it has more energy than it did before being hit by the photon. Chemists use an asterisk (*) to indicated that something is in an excited state. Thus, the collision of a photon with an electron (e) can be represented as follows:

$$e + h\nu \rightarrow e^*$$

Once an electron is excited, the whole atom in which it resides is also excited. Another way to represent the same change, then, is to show that the gold atom (Au) becomes excited when struck by a photon:

$$Au + h\nu \rightarrow Au^*$$

Emission of energy.   Electrons, atoms, and molecules normally do not remain in an excited state for very long. They tend to give off their excess energy very quickly and return to their original state. When they do so, they often undergo a chemical change. Since this change was originally made possible by absorbed light energy, it is known as a photochemical change.

The formation of ozone is just one example of the many kinds of photochemical changes that can occur. When solar energy breaks an oxygen molecule into two parts, one or both of the oxygen atoms formed may be excited. Another way to write the very first equation above is as follows:

$$O_2 + h\nu \rightarrow O^* + O$$

The excited oxygen atom (O^*) then has the excess energy needed to react with a second oxygen molecule to form ozone:

$$O^* + O_2 \rightarrow O_3$$

Another way for an excited atom or molecule to lose its energy is to give it off as light. This process is just the reverse of the process by which the atom or molecule first became excited. If the atom or molecule gives off its excess energy almost immediately, the material in which it is contained glows very briefly, a process known as fluorescence. If the excess energy is given off more slowly over a period of time, the process is known as phosphorescence. Both fluorescence and phosphorescence are examples of the general process of light emission by excited materials known as luminescence.

[*See also* **Atom; Luminescence; Photosynthesis**]

Photocopying

Photocopying is the process of photographically reproducing a document of text, illustrations, or other graphic matter. The most common photocopying method used today is called xerography (from the Greek words for "dry" and "writing").

The process of photocopying

The mechanics of photocopying is based on the principle of photoconductivity (when certain substances allow an electric current to flow through them when light is applied). For example, when light is absorbed by some of the electrons (particles that have a negative charge) that make up selenium (a nonmetallic chemical element that is used in the photocopying process), the electrons are able to pass from one atom to another

Words to Know

Electrostatics: Relating to painting with a spray that utilizes electrically charged particles to ensure a complete coating.

Toner: A material that carries an electrical charge opposite to that of a photoconducting surface that is added to that surface in a copy machine.

Xerography: A method of copying that uses dry powder, electric charge, and light to fuse an image onto paper.

when voltage is applied. When the light source is taken away, the electrons lose their mobility or ability to move.

During the process of photocopying, the round drum (usually made of aluminum) inside the copier is coated with a layer of selenium that is given a positive electrical charge. After placing the document to be copied on the glass-topped surface of the copier, a light exposes the image of the

Photocopiers are standard equipment found in most workplaces, and even some homes. *(Reproduced by permission of the Corbis Corporation [Bellevue].)*

document onto the drum. This causes the positive charge on the selenium-coated drum to fade except from the area to be copied. This area remains charged.

The negatively charged toner (ink) is then sprayed onto the drum, which forms an exact duplicate copy of the document. After that process is completed, a sheet of copy paper is passed by the drum at the same time that a positive electric charge is passed under the paper. The positive charge attracts the negatively charged toner image on the drum and the toner sticks in the same pattern onto the paper. Heat is quickly ap-

Chester Carlson demonstrating the first Xerox photocopier. *(Reproduced by permission of the Corbis Corporation [Bellevue].)*

plied to the copied image on the paper and it adheres the toner permanently to the paper.

Over the years, many improvements in the photocopying machine have taken place. Some enhancements include sorting and collating (arranging in order), enlarging or reducing the copied material, printing on both sides of the paper, and reproducing in color.

Inventor of photocopying

Xerography was invented by American physicist Chester F. Carlson (1906–1968) in 1938. After earning his physics degree from the California Institute of Technology in 1930, Carlson accepted a job working for the P.R. Mallory Company, an electronics business in New York. Working in the patent department, Carlson was frustrated by the difficulty of obtaining copies of patent drawings and specifications. He decided to use his time away from work to find a solution to the problem.

Focusing on the concept of electrostatics, Carlson spent four years before succeeding in production his first "dry-copy." The first successful copy was a notation of the date and location that read "10.-22.-38 Astoria." (Carlson lived in Astoria, Queens, New York at the time.) In 1940, Carlson obtained the first of many patents for his xerographic process. Wanting to find a company that would help him develop and market his idea, Carlson began showing his solution to many organizations. After more than twenty firms turned down his invention, Carlson finally reached an agreement in 1944 with the Battelle Memorial Institute, a nonprofit research organization. Three years later, the Haloid Company (later the Xerox Corporation) became a partner in the development of the xerography technology. Finally, after years of development, the first office copier—the Xerox 914—was introduced in 1959.

Photoelectric effect

When visible light, X rays, gamma rays, or other forms of electromagnetic radiation are shined on certain kinds of matter, electrons are ejected. That phenomenon is known as the photoelectric effect. The photoelectric effect was discovered by German physicist Heinrich Hertz (1857–1894) in 1887. You can imagine the effect as follows: Suppose that a metal plate is attached by two wires to a galvanometer. (A galvanometer is an instrument for measuring the flow of electric current.) If light of the cor-

Words to Know

Anode: The electrode in an electrochemical cell at which electrons are given up to a reaction.

Cathode: The electrode in an electrochemical cell at which electrons are taken up from a reaction.

Electrode: A material that will conduct an electrical current, usually a metal, used to carry electrons into or out of an electrochemical cell.

Electromagnetic radiation: Radiation (energy in the form of waves or subatomic particles) that transmits energy through the interaction of electricity and magnetism.

Frequency: The number of times a wave passes a given point in space per unit of time (as per second).

Photocell: A vacuum tube in which electric current flows when light strikes the photosensitive (or light sensitive) cathode.

Photon: A particle of light whose energy depends on its frequency.

Solar cell: A device constructed from specially prepared silicon that converts radiant energy (light) into electrical energy.

rect color is shined on the metal plate, the galvanometer may register a current. That reading indicates that electrons have been ejected from the metal plate. Those electrons then flow through the external wires and the galvanometer, providing the observed reading.

Photoelectric theory

The photoelectric effect is important in history because it caused scientists to think about light and other forms of electromagnetic radiation in a different way. The peculiar thing about the photoelectric effect is the relationship between the intensity of the light shined on a piece of metal and the amount of electric current produced.

To scientists, it seemed reasonable that you could make a stronger current flow if you shined a brighter light on the metal. More (or brighter) light should produce more electric current—or so everyone thought. But that isn't the case. For example, shining a very weak red light and a very strong red light on a piece of metal produces the same results. What does make a difference, though, is the *color* of the light used.

One way that scientists express the color of light is by specifying its frequency. The frequency of light and other forms of electromagnetic radiation is the number of times per second that light (or radiation) waves pass a given point. What scientists discovered was that light of some frequencies can produce an electric current, while light of other frequencies cannot.

Einstein's explanation. This strange observation was explained in 1905 by German-born American physicist Albert Einstein (1879–1955). Einstein hypothesized that light travels in the form of tiny packets of energy, now called photons. The amount of energy in each photon is equal to the frequency of light (ν) multiplied by a constant known as Planck's constant ($\hbar$), or $\nu\hbar$.

Einstein further suggested that electrons can be ejected from a material if they absorb exactly one photon of light, not a half photon, or a third photon, or some other fractional amount. Green light might not be effective in causing the photoelectric effect with some metals, Einstein said, because a photon of green light might not have exactly the right energy to eject an electron. But a photon of red light might have just the right amount of energy.

Einstein's explanation of the photoelectric effect was very important because it provided scientists with an alternative method of describing light. For centuries, researchers had thought of light as a form of energy that travels in waves. And that explanation works for many phenomena. But it does not work for phenomena such as the photoelectric effect and certain other properties of light.

Today, scientists have two different but complementary ways of describing light. In some cases, they say, it behaves like a wave. But in other cases, it behaves like a stream of particles—a stream of photons.

Applications

Two of the most important applications of the photoelectric effect are the photoelectric cell (or photocell) and solar cells. A photocell usually consists of a vacuum tube with two electrodes. A vacuum tube is a glass tube from which almost all of the air has been removed. The electrodes are two metal plates or wires. One electrode in a photocell consists of a metal (the cathode) that will emit electrons when exposed to light. The other electrode (the anode) is given a positive electric charge compared to the cathode. When light shines on the cathode, electrons are emitted and then attracted to the anode. An electron current flows in the tube from cathode to anode. The current can be used to turn on a motor, to open a door, or to ring a bell in an alarm system. The system can be made to respond to light, as described above, or it can be sensitive to the removal of light.

Photocells are commonly used in factories. Items on a conveyor belt pass between a beam of light and a photocell. As each item passes the beam, it interrupts the light, the current in the photocell stops, and a counter is turned on. With this method, the exact number of items leaving the factory can be counted. Photocells are also installed on light poles to turn street lights on and off at dusk and dawn. In addition, photocells are used as exposure meters in cameras. They measure the exact amount of light entering a camera, allowing a photographer to adjust the camera's lens to the correct setting.

Solar cells are devices for converting radiant energy (light) into electrical energy. They are usually made of specially prepared silicon that emits electrons when exposed to light. When a solar cell is exposed to sunlight, electrons emitted by silicon flow through external wires as a current.

Individual solar cells produce voltages of about 0.6 volts each. In most practical applications, higher voltages and large currents can be obtained by connecting many solar cells together. Electricity from solar cells is still quite expensive, but these cells remain very useful for providing small amounts of electricity in remote locations where other sources are not available. As the cost of producing solar cells is reduced, however, they will begin to be used for the production of large amounts of electricity for commercial use.

Photosynthesis

Photosynthesis is the process by which green plants and certain types of bacteria make carbohydrates, beginning only with carbon dioxide (CO_2) and water (H_2O). Carbohydrates are complex chemical compounds that occur widely in plants and that serve as an important food source for animals. Sugar, starch, and cellulose are among the most common carbohydrates. The energy needed to make photosynthesis possible comes from sunlight, which explains the term photo ("light") synthesis ("to

Words to Know

Carbohydrate: A compound consisting of carbon, hydrogen, and oxygen found in plants and used as a food by humans and other animals.

Chlorophyll: A compound in plants that makes possible the conversion of light energy to chemical energy.

Dark reactions: Those reactions in the photosynthesis process that can occur in the absence of sunlight.

Glucose: A sugar, or simple carbohydrate, that serves as an energy source for cells.

Light reactions: Those reactions in the photosynthesis process that can occur only in the presence of sunlight.

make"). The absorption of sunlight in plants takes place in specific molecules known as chlorophyll (KLOR-uh-fill) that give plants their green color.

Photosynthesis can be represented by means of a simple chemical equation:

$$6\ CO_2 + 6\ H_2O \xrightarrow[\text{chlorophyll}]{\text{light}} C_6H_{12}O_6 + 6\ O_2$$

In this equation, $C_6H_{12}O_6$ represents a simple sugar known as glucose. Molecules of glucose later combine with each other to form more complex carbohydrates, such as starch and cellulose. The oxygen formed during photosynthesis is released to the air. It is because of this oxygen that animal life on Earth is possible.

The stages of photosynthesis

The equation for photosynthesis shown above is very misleading. It suggests that changing carbon dioxide and water into carbohydrates is a simple, one-step process. Nothing could be further from the truth. Scientists have been working for well over 200 years trying to find out exactly what happens during photosynthesis. Although the major steps of the process are understood, researchers are still unable to duplicate the process in the laboratory.

The equation above seems to say that six carbon dioxide molecules (6 CO_2) and six water molecules (6 H_2O) somehow get joined to each other to form one carbohydrate molecule ($C_6H_{12}O_6$). Instead, the process occurs one small step at a time. During each of the many stages of photosynthesis, a single atom or an electron is transferred from one compound to another. Only after dozens of steps have taken place has the overall reaction shown above been completed.

What scientists have learned is that two general kinds of reactions are involved in photosynthesis: the light reactions and the dark reactions. Light reactions, as their name suggests, can take place only in the presence of sunlight. In those reactions, light energy is used to generate certain kinds of energy-rich compounds. These compounds do not themselves become part of the final carbohydrate product. Instead, they are used to "carry" energy from one compound to another in the process of photosynthesis.

The dark reactions are able to take place in the absence of sunlight, although they often occur during the daylight hours. During the dark reactions, the energy-rich compounds produced in the light reactions generate the compounds from which carbohydrates are eventually produced.

[*See also* **Plant**]

A transmission electron micrograph of a chloroplast from a tobacco leaf. Chloroplasts are the organelles in plants responsible for photosynthesis. *(Reproduced by permission of Photo Researchers, Inc.)*

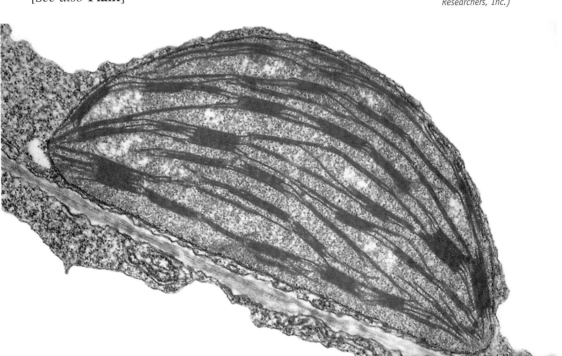

Phototropism

Phototropism (pronounced foe-TA-tro-piz-em) is the growth of a plant in the direction of its light source. Plants are very sensitive to their environment and have evolved many forms of "tropisms" in order to ensure their survival. A tropism is the growth of a plant as a response to a stimulus, and phototropism occurs when a plant responds to light by bending in the direction of the light. Although plant physiologists (scientists who study how the processes of a plant actually work) know that this growth is caused by a plant hormone, they still do not fully understand exactly how it works.

Bending toward the light

Most of us at some time have noticed a houseplant on a windowsill that seems to have all of its thin stems leaning in the same direction, as if it were trying to press itself against the glass. Picking it up and turning the entire pot in the opposite direction so that the plant is pointing away from the window will only result, about eight hours later, in the plant having reversed itself and going about its business of pointing its leaves toward the window again. This is not because plants especially like

Plants respond to the direction and amount of light they receive. The seedlings on the left grew toward the light it received on only one side. The plant in the center received no light. The plant on the right was grown in normal, all-around light. *(Reproduced by permission of Photo Researchers, Inc.)*

Words to Know

Auxin: Any of various hormones or similar synthetic substances that regulate the growth and development of plants.

Photosynthesis: Chemical process by which plants containing chlorophyll use sunlight to manufacture their own food by converting carbon dioxide and water to carbohydrates, releasing oxygen as a by-product.

Tropism: The growth or movement of a plant toward or away from a stimulus.

windows but rather because light is essential to their survival, and they have developed ways of making sure they get all they need.

We know then that it is the light coming through the window that the plants are striving to get closer to, but how is a plant, which is rooted in soil, able to "move" toward the light? Actually, the plant does not so much move toward the light source as it grows in that direction. As already noted, this growth of a plant that occurs as a response to a stimulus is called a tropism. There are several forms of tropisms, such as gravitropism or geotropism, in which a plant reacts to the force of gravity; hydrotropism, in which the presence of water causes a response; galvanotropism, in which a plant reacts to a direct electrical current; thigmotropism, in which a plant responds to being touched or some form of contact; and chemotropism, in which a plant reacts to a chemical stimulus. Since the prefix "photo" refers to light, phototropism involves a plant responding to light. In all of these tropisms, the plant's response involves some form of growth. Finally, all tropisms are either positive or negative, although these words are not always used. So when a plant's leaves grow toward the light (stimulus), it is technically called positive phototropism. When its roots normally grow away from the light, it is called negative phototropism.

How phototropism works

It is known that as long ago as 1809, Swiss botanist Augustin Pyrame de Candolle (1778–1841) observed the growth of a plant toward the light and stated that it was caused by an unequal growth on only one part of the plant. However, he could not understand how this was happening.

Some seventy years later, English naturalist Charles Darwin (1809–1882) began to grow canary grass in order to feed the birds he kept, and he eventually discovered that it was the tips of the sprouting seedlings that were influenced by the direction of their light source. He and his son Francis learned this when they covered the tips of some seedlings and found that they did not move toward the light. When only the seedlings' stems were covered, however, they still moved toward the light.

It was not until the 1920s that Dutch botanist Frits W. Went (1903–1990) proved the connection between phototropism and a plant hormone called auxin. Went discovered that plants manufacture a growth stimulant (which he named auxin) in their tips, which they then send to other cells in the plant. In phototropism, however, this growth hormone is distributed unevenly when the light source comes from only one direction. Specifically, more auxin flows down the dark side, meaning that it grows faster than the exposed side of the plant. This unequal or one-sided growth (also called differential growth) brings about the curving or bending of the plant toward the light source. Went named this growth hormone after the Greek word *auxein,* which means "to increase." Although it was isolated and named, auxin was not understood chemically until twenty years later when it was finally identified chemically as indole-3-acetic acid.

Plants can react and adjust

Understanding what plant tropism is and, specifically, what happens during phototropism makes us realize that plants, as living things, necessarily demonstrate the several characteristics of life. Specifically, this includes growth, response to stimuli, and adaptation. It is because of its hormones that a plant's stem always grows upwards and its roots always grown downward. Since plants must make their own food to survive (by changing light energy into chemical energy—a process called photosynthesis), the ability to capture as much of this light energy as possible is crucial to its survival. Thus, plants have developed a chemical response to light or the lack of it that causes their stems to bend toward the stronger light.

Today, we know that a certain minimal amount of light (whether natural or artificial) has to be present for the plant to react chemically. This is called its threshold value. Despite our understanding of the basic stages and phases of phototropism, we are only now beginning to obtain the most basic knowledge of what goes on at the genetic and molecular level. We do realize however that plants are living, sensitive things that can adjust to their environment and actually seek out the light they need if they are not getting enough.

[*See also* **Plant**]

Physical therapy

Physical therapy is the use of exercise, heat, cold, water, massage, or electricity in the treatment of damaged muscles, bones, or joints due to injury or disease. The goal of physical therapy is to restore full or partial function of the affected body part or to build up other muscles to make up for weak ones. Physical therapy is usually performed by a trained physical therapist, who sets up a therapy program based on instructions from a medical doctor.

Types of physical therapy

Mechanical manipulation.   Massage, manipulation of the injured limb, weight lifting, and water therapy are mechanical forms of physical therapy. Massage is the rubbing, tapping, or kneading of an injured area to increase blood circulation and relieve pain. Manipulation consists of manually bending an injured joint to restore full range of motion and eliminate pain from movement. Weight lifting involves the use of machines or free weights to strengthen and build muscle. Water therapy includes walking or exercising in water and using the resistance it provides to build muscle and increase range of motion of joints.

A physical therapist and patient in a water therapy pool. The patient has plastic attachments on his hands and feet that resist movement through the water, allowing him to build strength and flexibility. *(Reproduced by permission of Photo Researchers, Inc.)*

▼ Words to Know

Conversion: Process by which sound waves or electric currents passed through the skin are transformed into heat.

Diathermy: The production of heat in body tissue through the use of electric currents.

Iontophoresis: The administration of a drug through the skin by an electric current.

TENS (transcutaneous electrical nerve stimulation): The use of electric currents passed through the skin to relieve pain in a specific area of the body.

Ultrasound: A technique in which high-frequency sound waves raise the temperature of body tissue by producing vibrations within it.

Cold therapy. Cold therapy is an effective means of reducing tissue inflammation following an injury or surgery. Cold therapy is applied in the form of ice packs, sometimes combined with massage or a cold water bath of the injured area. The cold temperature reduces blood flow to the injured site, reducing inflammation and bleeding. Oxygen demand of the injured tissue is decreased, preserving the muscle cells. In addition, the anesthetic effect of the cold temperature helps to ease pain.

Heat therapy. Heat therapy may be used after active swelling of an injury has stopped, usually within 24 to 48 hours. Heat can be applied with moist heat packs, hot water (as in a whirlpool bath), a heat lamp, or by conversion. Conversion is the generation of heat by the passage of sound waves or electric currents through tissue. Diathermy is an example of electric currents directed into tissue and converted into heat. Ultrasound is a technique that uses high-frequency sound waves to heat joints, which can help to relieve joint pain.

Heat increases blood flow to the area, which helps to reduce muscle spasms, increases the amount of oxygen reaching the injured tissue, and carries waste products from the site.

Electrical stimulation. The application of electricity can restore muscle tone by stimulating muscles to contract rhythmically. This method is often used to exercise the muscles of a person confined to a wheelchair or bed. Over time, muscles that are not used will atrophy (become smaller and weaker). The application of electrical stimulation can prevent muscle atrophy in wheelchair-bound patients and reduce the length of therapy required for patients who regain mobility.

Electricity also can be used to drive molecules of medication through the skin into the tissues. This is called iontophoresis. Pain caused by an injury or illness (such as cancer) can be controlled using TENS (transcutaneous electrical nerve stimulation). A TENS machine passes electric current through the skin (transcutaneously) of the injured or diseased site, stimulating certain nerve fibers and blocking the transmission of pain impulses through others.

Physics

Physics is the science that deals with matter and energy and with the interaction between them. Perhaps you would like to determine how best to aim a rifle in order to hit a target with a bullet. Or you want to know how to build a ship out of steel and make sure that it will float. Or you plan to design a house that can be heated just with sunlight. Physics can be used in answering any of these questions.

Physics is one of the oldest of the sciences. It is usually said to have begun with the work of Italian scientist Galileo Galilei (1564–1642) in the first half of the seventeenth century. Galileo laid down a number of basic rules as to how information about the natural world should be collected. For example, the only way to obtain certain knowledge about the natural world, he said, is to carry out controlled observations (experiments) that will lead to measurable quantities. The fact that physics today is based on careful experimentation, measurements, and systems of mathematical analysis reflects the basic teachings of Galileo.

Classical and modern physics

The field of physics is commonly subdivided into two large categories: classical and modern physics. The dividing line between these two subdivisions can be drawn in the early 1900s. During that period, a number of revolutionary new concepts about the nature of matter were proposed. Included among these concepts were Einstein's theories of general and special relativity, Planck's concept of the quantum, Heisenberg's principle of indeterminacy, and the concept of the equivalence of matter and energy.

Words to Know

Determinism: The notion that a known effect can be attributed with certainty to a known cause.

Energy: The ability to do work.

Matter: Anything that has mass and takes up space.

Mechanics: The science that deals with energy and forces and their effects on bodies.

Submicroscopic: Levels of matter that cannot be directly observed by the human senses, even with the best of instruments; the level of atoms and electrons.

In general, classical physics can be said to deal with topics on the macroscopic scale, that is on a scale that can be studied with the largely unaided five human senses. Modern physics, in contrast, concerns the nature and behavior of particles and energy at the submicroscopic level. The term submicroscopic refers to objects—such as atoms and electrons—that are too small to be seen even with the very best microscope. One of the interesting discoveries made in the early 1900s was that the laws of classical physics generally do not hold true at the submicroscopic level.

Perhaps the most startling discovery made during the first two decades of the twentieth century concerned causality. Causality refers to the belief in cause-and-effect; that is, classical physics taught that if A occurs, B is certain to follow. For example, if you know the charge and mass of an electron, you can calculate its position in an atom. This kind of cause-and-effect relationship was long regarded as one of the major pillars of physics.

What physicists learned in the early twentieth century is that nature is not really that predictable. One could no longer be certain that A would always cause B. Instead, physicists began talking about probability, the likelihood that A would cause B. In drawing pictures of atoms, for example, physicists could no longer talk about the path that electrons *do* take in atoms. Instead, they began to talk about the paths that electrons *probably* take (with a 95 percent or 90 percent or 80 percent probability).

Divisions of physics

Like other fields of science, physics is commonly subdivided into a number of more specific fields of research. In classical physics, those fields include mechanics; thermodynamics; sound, light, and optics; and electricity and magnetism. In modern physics, some major subdivisions include atomic, nuclear, high-energy, and particle physics.

The classical divisions. Mechanics is the oldest field of physics. It is concerned with the description of motion and its causes. Many of the basic concepts of mechanics grew out of the work of English physicist Isaac Newton (1642–1727) in about 1687. Thermodynamics sprang from efforts to develop an efficient steam engine in the early 1800s. The field deals with the nature of heat and its connection with work.

Sound, optics, electricity, and magnetism are all divisions of physics in which the nature and movement of waves are important. The study of sound is also related to practical applications that can be made of this form of energy, as in radio communication and human speech. Similarly, optics deals not only with the reflection, refraction, diffraction, interference, polarization, and other properties of light, but also with the ways in which these principles have practical applications in the design of tools and instruments such as telescopes and microscopes.

The study of electricity and magnetism focuses on the properties of particles at rest *and* on the properties of those particles in motion. Thus, the field of static electricity examines the forces that exist between charged particles at rest, while current electricity deals with the movement of electrical particles.

The modern divisions. In the area of modern physics, nuclear and atomic physics involve the study of the atomic nucleus and its parts, with special attention to changes that take place (such as nuclear decay) in the atom. Particle and high-energy physics, on the other hand, focus on the nature of the fundamental particles of which the natural world is made. In these two fields of research, very powerful, very expensive tools such as linear accelerators and synchrotrons (atom-smashers) are required to carry out the necessary research.

Interrelationship of physics to other sciences

One trend in all fields of science over the past century has been to explore ways in which the five basic sciences (physics, chemistry, astronomy, biology, and earth sciences) are related to each other. This trend has led to another group of specialized sciences in which the laws of physics are used to interpret phenomena in other fields. Astrophysics, for example, is a study of the composition of astronomical objects—such as stars—and the changes that they undergo. Physical chemistry and chemical physics, on the other hand, are fields of research that deal with the physical nature of chemical molecules. Biophysics, as another example, is concerned with the physical properties of molecules essential to living organisms.

[*See also* **Quantum mechanics; Relativity, theory of**]

Physiology

Physiology is the branch of biology that deals with the functions of living organisms and the parts of which they are made. This scientific discipline covers a wide variety of functions, ranging from the cellular and below to the interaction of organ systems that keep the most complex biological machines running.

Some of the questions that physiologists investigate include how plants grow, how bacteria divide, how food is processed in various organisms, and how thought processes occur in the brain. Investigations in physiology often lead to a better understanding of the origins of diseases.

History of physiology

Human (or mammalian) physiology is the oldest branch of this science. It dates back to at least 420 B.C. and the time of Hippocrates, the father of medicine. Modern physiology first appeared in the seventeenth century when scientific methods of observation and experimentation were used to study the movement of blood in the body. In 1929, American physiologist W. B. Cannon coined the term homeostasis to describe one of the most basic concerns of physiology: how the varied components of living things adjust to maintain a constant internal environment that makes possible optimal functioning.

A number of technological advances, ranging from the simple microscope to ultra-high-technology computerized scanning devices, contributed to the growth of physiology. No longer confined to investigating the functioning components of life that could be observed with the naked eye, physiologists began to delve into the most basic life-forms, like bacteria. They could also study organisms' basic molecular functions, such as the electrical potentials in cells that help control heart beat.

Words to Know

Homeostasis: The tendency of an organism to maintain constant internal conditions despite large changes in the external environment.

Negative feedback loop: A homeostatic mechanism that opposes or resists a change in the body's internal conditions.

Set point: The range of normal values of an organ or structure.

Branches of physiology

The branches of physiology are almost as varied as the countless life-forms that inhabit Earth. Viral physiology, for example, focuses on how viruses feed, grow, reproduce, and excrete by-products. However, the more complex an organism, the more avenues of research open to the physiologist. Human physiology, for instance, is concerned with the functioning of organs, like the heart and liver, and how the senses, such as sight and smell, work.

Physiologists also observe and analyze how certain body systems, like the circulatory, respiratory, and nervous systems, work independently and together to maintain life. This branch of physiology is known as comparative physiology. Ecological physiology, on the other hand, studies how animals developed or evolved specific biological mechanisms to cope with a particular environment. An example is the trait of dark skin, which provides protection against harmful rays of the Sun for humans who live in tropical climates. Cellular physiology, or cell biology, focuses on the structures and functions of the cell. Like cell biology, many branches of physiology are better known by other names, including biochemistry, biophysics, and endocrinology (the study of secreting tissues).

Homeostasis

A fundamental principle of physiology is homeostasis. Homeostasis is the tendency of an organism to maintain constant internal conditions despite large changes in the external environment. Most organisms can survive only if certain vital functions are maintained within a relatively narrow range. Such functions include blood pressure, body temperature, respiration rate, and blood glucose (sugar) levels. The normal range of values for any one of these functions is called a set point. Homeostasis insures that vital functions remain close to their set point in spite of any changes in external conditions.

For instance, suppose that a child leaves a warm house to go outside to play when the temperature is 32°F (0°C). When that happens, the homeostatic mechanisms in the child's body begin to make adjustments for this change in external temperature. It "turns on" chemical reactions inside the body that result in the generation of body heat, thereby maintaining its internal temperature at constant levels.

Negative feedback. The primary mechanism by which homeostasis occurs in an organism is called negative feedback. The term negative feedback means that any change that takes place is resisted by the body. In the example above, for instance, a decrease in the external temperature causes biological and chemical changes that produce an increase in internal temperatures. Or, suppose that a person suffers an accident and his or her blood pressure begins to drop. Systems within the body then respond to that emergency by producing an increase in blood pressure.

[*See also* **Brain; Circulatory system; Disease; Nervous system; Reproductive system**]

Plague

Plague is an infectious, deadly disease caused by the bacterium *Yersinia pestis*. Plague pandemics (outbreaks of disease over a wide geographic area and affecting a large number of people) have wiped out populations since A.D. 542. Today, plague is sometimes seen in parts of the western United States and remains present in certain regions of the world including South America, Mexico, and parts of Asia and Africa.

Transmission of plague

Plague is normally transmitted to humans by the bite of a flea that has ingested blood from an infected rodent, such as a rat, squirrel, or prairie dog. Transmission from person to person usually occurs only if a person's lungs become infected, in which case the disease is highly contagious and can be transmitted to others easily through a cough or sneeze.

Forms of plague

In humans, plague can take three forms. Bubonic plague usually results from a flea bite and is characterized by swollen lymph glands called buboes that are extremely painful and that give this form its name. Other symptoms include fever, muscle aches, and weakness. Hemorrhaging (heavy bleeding) under the skin can result in patches of dead tissue that appear black. (Hence, this disease is sometimes referred to as the Black Death.) If not treated, bubonic plague has a death rate of about 60 percent, meaning three out of every five people who contract it will die.

In another form of plague, called septicemia plague, bacteria enter the blood and cause infection throughout the body. This is a rapidly fatal form that usually results in death within two days if not immediately treated.

A third form, called pneumonic plague, occurs when the bacteria infect the lungs. Pneumonic plague results in pneumonia and is highly contagious. It also usually causes death within two or three days of the initial infection if left untreated.

Plague pandemics

The most famous bubonic plague pandemic occurred in the fourteenth century in Europe and parts of Asia. Called the Black Death, this pandemic was caused by infected rats carried to Europe in trading ships. It killed about one-third of Europe's population. Because it caused so many deaths, this particular outbreak of plague had a major impact on the economy and political structure of Europe.

Burning of houses during the last worldwide outbreak of the plague in the 1890s. The disease spread from China westward along trade routes. *(Reproduced by permission of Photo Researchers, Inc.)*

A plague pandemic that began in Burma in 1894 spread to China through Hong Kong, and then to North and South America. During this pandemic, the United States saw its first outbreak of plague, occurring in San Francisco in 1900. In 1994, an outbreak of plague in India killed 56 people and caused widespread panic.

Prevention

Plague pandemics can be prevented by disinfecting ships, aircraft, and persons who are known to be infected with the disease. The classic route of transmission that leads to pandemics is the transportation of infected rodents aboard transcontinental vehicles. Since many countries have rigorous procedures for disinfection of ships and planes, plague cases have dropped dramatically. Control of rodent populations in cities is an additional means of preventing plague outbreaks.

If a person is diagnosed with plague, most countries, including the United States, require that the government health agency be notified. The person is usually kept under strict quarantine (in isolation) until the disease is brought under control with antibiotics.

Plankton

Plankton are microscopic plants and small animals that live in the surface waters of oceans, lakes, and rivers and drift with the currents. They include bacteria, fungi, algae, protozoa, invertebrates, and some vertebrates.

Phytoplankton are photosynthetic, meaning that they use sunlight to convert carbon dioxide and water into organic molecules such as glucose to use as food. Phytoplankton include microscopic algae, blue-green bac-

Words to Know

Algae: Single-celled or multicellular plants or plantlike organisms that contain chlorophyll.

Bacteria: Single-celled microorganisms that live in soil, water, plants, and animals, and some of which are agents of disease.

Consumer: Organisms that cannot make their own food and consume other organisms to obtain the nutrients they need for growth.

Ecosystem: A community of organisms—plants, animals, and microorganisms—together with their environment.

Food chain: A series of organisms, each dependent on the organism at the level below it for food.

Food web: An interconnected set of all the food chains in the same ecosystem.

Fungi: Kingdom of various single-celled or multicellular organisms, including mushrooms, molds, yeasts, and mildews, that do not contain chlorophyll.

Invertebrates: Animals that lack backbones.

Photosynthesis: Chemical process by which plants containing chlorophyll use sunlight to manufacture their own food by converting carbon dioxide and water to carbohydrates, releasing oxygen as a by-product.

Primary producer: Organisms such as plants, algae, and certain bacteria that make organic molecules from inorganic substances.

Protozoa: Single-celled animal-like microscopic organisms that must live in the presence of water.

Vertebrates: Animals with backbones.

teria, and some true bacteria. These organisms exist in waters where light is able to penetrate. Phytoplankton form the base of nearly all aquatic food chains, directly or indirectly supplying the energy needed by most aquatic protozoa and animals.

Zooplankton are small grazing animals that live in surface waters and feed on phytoplankton. The amount of zooplankton present in a given area depends on the amount of the microscopic algae present. Zooplankton are a diverse group mostly made up of crustaceans (animals with external skeletons) such as water fleas and shrimps but also include jellyfish, protozoa, and insects. Some species of zooplankton are predators, feeding on other species of zooplankton, and some spend part of their lives as parasites of larger animals, such as fish.

Zooplankton are very important in open-water marine and freshwater food webs. They are eaten by relatively small fish that are then eaten by larger fish. Zooplankton are an important link in the transfer of energy from the algae (the primary producers) to the ecologically and economically important fish community (the consumers).

Species of zooplankton react differently to factors that place stress on aquatic ecosystems. Toxic chemicals, acidity of the water, decreased oxygen, or changes in temperature may kill some zooplankton while others survive. As a result, the health of a body of water or a change in its physical or chemical makeup can be determined in part by the species of zooplankton that are present.

[*See also* **Crustaceans; Protozoa**]

Plant

A plant is any organism in the kingdom Plantae. Kingdoms are the main divisions into which scientists classify all living things on Earth. The other kingdoms are: Monera (single-celled organisms without nuclei), Protista (single-celled organisms with a nucleus), Fungi, and Animalia (animals). The scientific study of plants is called botany.

A general definition of a plant is any organism that contains chlorophyll (a green pigment contained in a specialized cell called a chloroplast) and can manufacture its own food. Another characteristic of plants is that their rigid cell walls are composed mainly of cellulose, a complex carbohydrate that is insoluble (cannot be dissolved) in water. Because of the vast number of plants that exist, cellulose is the most abundant organic compound on Earth. Biologists have identified about 500,000 species of plants, although there are many undiscovered species, especially in tropical rain forests.

Plant structure

Those plants that produce seeds are the dominant and most studied group of plants on the planet. The leaves of these plants are all covered

Words to Know

Carbohydrate: A compound consisting of carbon, hydrogen, and oxygen found in plants and used as a food by humans and other animals.

Chlorophyll: Green pigment found in chloroplasts that absorbs sunlight, providing the energy used in photosynthesis.

Chloroplasts: Small structures in plant cells that contain chlorophyll and in which the process of photosynthesis takes place.

Meristem: Special plant tissues that contain actively growing and dividing cells.

Phloem: Plant tissue consisting of elongated cells that transport carbohydrates and other nutrients.

Photosynthesis: Process by which sunlight is used by plants to form carbohydrates from carbon dioxide and water, releasing oxygen as a by-product.

Stomata: Pores in the surface of leaves.

Transpiration: Evaporation of water in the form of water vapor from the stomata.

Xylem: Plant tissue consisting of elongated cells that transport water and mineral nutrients.

with a cuticle, a waxy layer that inhibits water loss. The leaves have stomata, microscopic pores, that open during the day to take in carbon dioxide and release oxygen during photosynthesis (process by which sunlight is used to form carbohydrates from carbon dioxide and water, releasing oxygen as a by-product).

Leaves are connected to the stem by veins, which transport water and nutrients throughout the plant. There are two special types of cells in this vascular system (the vessels that carry water and nutrients): xylem and phloem. Xylem (pronounced ZEYE-lem) are mainly responsible for the movement of water and minerals from the roots to the stems and leaves. Phloem (pronounced FLOW-em) are mainly responsible for the transport of food, principally carbohydrates produced by photosynthesis, from the leaves throughout the plant. The vascular system of plants differs from the circulatory system of animals in that water (in the form of vapor) evaporates out of a plant's stomata (a process called transpiration), whereas an animal's blood is recirculated throughout the body.

The roots of a plant take up water and minerals from the soil, and also anchor the plant. Most plants have a dense, fibrous network of roots, and this provides a large surface area for the uptake of water and minerals.

Plant development

As a plant grows, it undergoes developmental changes. Most plants continually produce new sets of organs, such as leaves, flowers, and fruits. In contrast, animals typically develop their organs only once and these organs merely increase in size as the animal grows.

A plant begins its life as a seed. Various environmental cues such as sunlight, temperature changes, and the presence of nutrients signal a seed to germinate (grow). During early germination, the young seedling depends upon nutrients stored within the seed itself for growth. As the seedling grows, it begins to produce chlorophyll and turn green. Most plants become green only when exposed to sunlight because the production of chlorophyll is light-induced.

In contrast to animals, whose bodies grow all over as they develop, plants generally grow in specific regions, referred to as meristems. A

Leaves of a nerve plant (*Fittonia verschaffeltii*). (Reproduced by permission of Field Mark Publications.)

meristem is a special tissue that contains actively growing and dividing cells. Apical meristems are at the tips of shoots and roots and are responsible for elongation of a plant. Lateral meristems are located along the outer sides of the stem of a plant and are responsible for thickening of the plant.

Plant diseases

Plant diseases can be infectious (transmitted from plant to plant) or noninfectious. Noninfectious diseases are usually referred to as disorders. Common plant disorders are caused by a shortage of plant nutrients, by waterlogged or polluted soil, and by polluted air. Too little (or too much) water or improper nutrition can cause plants to grow poorly. Plants can also be stressed by weather that is too hot or too cold, by too little or too much light, and by heavy winds. Pollution from automobiles and industry and the excessive use of herbicides (to kill weeds) can also cause noninfectious plant disorders.

Infectious plant diseases are caused by living microorganisms that infect a plant and rob it of nutrients. Bacteria, fungi, and viruses are the living agents that cause plant diseases. None of these microorganisms are visible to the naked eye, but the diseases they cause can be detected by the symptoms of wilting, yellowing, stunting, and abnormal growth patterns.

Some plant diseases are caused by rod-shaped bacteria. The bacteria enter the plant through natural openings, like the stomata of the leaves, or through wounds in the plant tissue. Once inside, the bacteria plug up the plant's vascular system and cause the plant to wilt. Other common symptoms of bacterial disease include rotting and swollen plant tissues. Bacteria can be spread by water, insects, infected soil, or contaminated tools.

About 80 percent of plant diseases can be traced to fungi, which can grow on living or dead plant tissue. They can penetrate plant tissue or grow on the plant's surface. Fungal spores, which act like seeds, are spread by wind, water, soil, and animals to other plants. Warm, humid conditions promote fungal growth.

Viruses are the hardest pathogens (disease-causing organisms) to control. Destroying the infected plants to prevent spreading to healthy plants is usually the best control method. While more than 300 plant viruses have been identified, new strains continually appear because these organisms are capable of mutating (changing their genetic makeup). Viruses are spread by contaminated seeds and sucking insects (aphids, leafhoppers, thrips) that act as carriers of the virus. The symptoms of viral infection include yellowing, stunted growth in some part of the plant. Leaf rolls and narrow leaf growth are other indications of viral infection. The mosaic viruses can infect many plants. Plants infected with this virus have mottled or streaked leaves.

Scientists complete first planet genetic sequence

In the nineteenth century, Austrian botanist Gregor Mendel (1822–1884) started the science of genetics when he studied the genetic charac-

Smut—a fungus—on corn. About 80 percent of plant diseases can be traced to fungi. *(Reproduced by permission of Photo Researchers, Inc.)*

teristics of pea plants. Over 100 years later, in late 2000, scientists from the United States, Europe, and Japan determined the first complete genetic sequence of a plant. Fellow scientists hailed the accomplishment, saying it would deepen understanding of plant biology and provide new ways to engineer crops genetically to increase food production and improve nutrition. The planet, commonly called thale cress, is a small weed that is related to the mustard plant. It is worthless as a crop. However, like a laboratory mouse, it is being studied for insights that can be applied to virtually all other plants. As a matter of fact, scientists are testing genes found in the plant to make other plants flower more quickly, to keep fruits from ripening too early, and to produce healthier vegetable oils. Scientists have already identified 100 genes in the thale cress that can be used to design new herbicides.

[*See also* **Cellulose; Flower; Photosynthesis; Phototropism; Seeds**]

Plastic surgery

Plastic surgery is the branch of medicine concerned with the reconstruction and repair of defects in the body. Reconstructive plastic surgery repairs deformities or disfigurements caused by injuries, disease, or birth defects. It seeks not only to make a person look more normal but to function better as well. Cosmetic plastic surgery is performed solely for the purpose of improving the appearance of the body.

Origin of name

Many people have the mistaken belief that plastic surgery got its name because it involves the use of some sort of plastic or other man-made material. In fact, the term plastic surgery comes from the Greek word "plastikos," which means to mold or to shape. The first published use of that word was by German surgeon Karl Ferdinand von Graefe (1787–1840), one of the pioneers of plastic surgery. Von Graefe operated on the cleft palate (a birth defect in the roof of the mouth) and the eye and developed the first satisfactory procedure to correct the nose, called rhinoplasty (pronounced RYE-no-pla-stee), which he described in his 1818 book *Rhinoplastik*.

However, von Graefe was by no means the first or the earliest to perform such surgery. In fact, many believe that plastic surgery is one of the oldest forms of surgery. Some say that the earliest known surgery of any type dates back to the Peruvians of about 10,000 B.C., who performed

Words to Know

Cosmetic plastic surgery: Surgery designed primarily to enhance or improve the looks of an individual who may not have a gross deformity or physical impairment.

Graft: Bone, skin, or other tissue taken from one place on the body (or from another body) and then transplanted to another place on that body where it begins to grow again.

Reconstructive plastic surgery: Surgery designed to restore the normal appearance and functioning of disfigured or impaired areas of the human body.

craniotomies (pronounced kray-nee-AH-toh-meez) or surgery on the skull by burning holes in a person's head. Many of the healed skulls of these patients have been found, suggesting that they survived the operation.

Ancient surgery

Reconstructive plastic surgery is less old, although there is written evidence that surgeons in ancient India used skin grafts as early as 3300 B.C. to repair noses and ears lost in battle or to certain forms of punishment. Roman medical writer Aulus Cornelius Celsus, who is known to have lived during the reign of Tiberius (A.D. 14–37), mentioned the reconstructive surgery of the face in his book *De re medicina.* It is also known that during the Chin dynasty (A.D. 229–317), Chinese surgeons surgically repaired cleft lips.

While surgical techniques developed slowly for many centuries up to the Renaissance (a period of vigorous artistic and intellectual activity that began in Italy in the fourteenth century and soon spread across Europe, lasting into the seventeenth century), the first textbook on plastic surgery was written by Italian surgeon Gasparo Tagliacozzi (1546–1599). His book *De curatorum chirurgia* contained illustrations as well as words on how to surgically repair or correct the nose. One famous image in that book shows how he placed his patients in a type of straight-jacket in which one of their hands was placed on the back of their head with their nose touching their shoulder or bicep. In this way he used the patient's own skin (on the arm) to graft new skin to the repaired nose.

Wartime advances

Surgical techniques continued to progress very slowly, yet in 1775, American surgeon John Jones (1729–1791) published the first surgical textbook in the American colonies, *Plain, Concise, Practical Remarks on the Treatment of Wounds and Fractures.* This book introduced plastic surgery techniques to the American colonies and became the military surgeon's bible when the Revolutionary War (1775–81) broke out. However, the first American plastic surgeon is considered to be Virginia surgeon John Peter Mettauer (1787–1875). By the time Mettauer had performed his first cleft palate operation in 1827, progress also was being made in Europe as surgeons in Italy and Germany performed skin graft experiments on animals. In the United States, the battles of the Civil War (1861–65) produced large numbers of injured and disfigured soldiers, and many surgical techniques were discovered or developed out of necessity.

Finally, it took another war, World War I (1914–18), to produce the father of modern plastic surgery, British surgeon Harold Delf Gillies (1882–1960). Since this war was conducted mostly in trenches, there were huge numbers of head and face injuries (since the rest of a soldier's body was usually below ground level and therefore protected). Gillies established the first hospital devoted to reconstructive surgery, and in 1917, he introduced the pedicle (pronounced PED-ih-kul) type of skin graft that uses the patient's own skin and the tissue below it to nourish the repaired site. Many of his discoveries and techniques formed the basics of modern plastic surgery. By World War II (1939–45), many of the armed forces had plastic surgeons as part of their medical teams, and following the war, microsurgical techniques had advanced to the point where the public became aware of cosmetic surgery as a way of enhancing their appearance.

Reconstructive plastic surgery

Today, plastic surgery has two components: reconstructive plastic surgery and cosmetic plastic surgery. Reconstructive surgery does just what it sounds like, since it reconstructs, repairs, or reshapes abnormal structures of the body. In other words, its goal is to fix things or to restore the function (as well as the appearance) of a body part that may have been injured, diseased, or suffered from some birth defect. Repairs of severe lacerations (deep cuts) and compound bone fractures are typical procedures, as are tissue grafts to repair severe burns. Removing cancerous skin growths and rebuilding lost or deformed parts, such as an ear or a nose, are other examples of reconstructive plastic surgery. The goal is always to restore damaged function by restoring normal form. It is this type of surgery that attempts to reattach severed fingers and limbs and to correct the damage done by the trauma of injury or disease.

Cosmetic plastic surgery

Cosmetic plastic surgery is the other type of plastic surgery. Also called aesthetic plastic surgery, it differs from reconstructive plastic surgery in that it is surgery performed on normal structures of the body. In other words, it is surgery performed solely for the purpose of improving the appearance of an otherwise healthy person. Examples of such operations would be "nose jobs," "face lifts," breast enlargement, and fat-suctioning procedures. This type of surgery is called "elective" because it is not necessary from a medical point of view. Rather, it is done to improve a person's self-image by fixing something that person finds objectionable about his or her body. Thus, while some choose to have their large ears put closer to their heads, others may elect to have the drooping skin around their eyes tightened or the wrinkles in their face removed. Hair transplants and chemical face peeling are also considered cosmetic plastic surgery.

Grafting

A silicone breast implant. *(Reproduced by permission of The Stock Market.)*

Whether reconstructive or cosmetic, plastic surgery is almost always about tissue transplantation. However, this is not surgery that

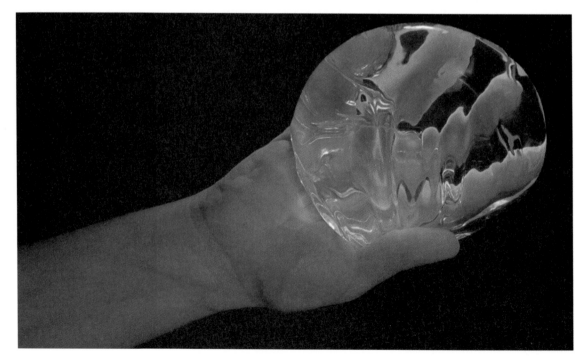

"transplants" a working donor organ like a kidney into someone who has lost theirs, but instead is the transplantation or grafting of healthy tissue from one part of the body to replace damaged tissue removed from another part. This tissue could be bone, skin, muscle, cartilage, tendons, or even nerves. Thus a surgeon can take cartilage from a patient's rib and "build" an ear or fix a nose. Baseball pitchers sometimes resume their throwing careers after having cartilage taken from their non-throwing arm surgically transplanted into their injured throwing elbow. Skin grafts used to cover a burned area are another common form of transplantation. A new version of this is called a xenograft (pronounced ZEE-no-graft), in which skin from a donor is used temporarily and grafted to a burned area that still has living cells. Although it is eventually rejected, the grafted skin often protects the damaged tissue just long enough, and gives the body time to heal itself. An even newer form of artificial or synthetic skin is being developed that will do the same thing.

Recent advances

Another essential part of all plastic surgery, whether reconstructive or cosmetic, is the planned and careful cutting of the skin in places where it follows or falls in the skin's natural lines or folds. At the end of surgery, an equally planned and careful way of suturing (pronounced SOO-chur-ing) or sewing the wound closed is necessary. Today, plastic surgeons sometimes use lasers instead of scalpels, and often perform an entire operation at such a fine level of detail that they use a microscope the entire time. They can reattach the smallest of blood vessels using this technology. Even before they operate, they have access to such diagnostic technologies as magnetic resonance imaging and computed tomography that allow them to analyze and understand the problem better, and to plan how to repair it.

Despite the increased popularity of cosmetic plastic surgery (it is no longer a luxury only for the rich), reconstructive plastic surgery is still performed three times as often. Corrective eye surgery or blepharoplasty (pronounced BLEH-fer-oh-plas-tee)—in which bags under the eyes or skin on the upper eyelids are removed to give a person a younger, less tired look—is the most common type of cosmetic surgery. Hair transplants and eye surgery are the most popular procedures with men. Many adult women choose breast augmentation, now done with saline or salt water implants instead of the proven-dangerous silicone implants. Teenagers most often receive nose reshaping.

[*See also* **Surgery**]

Plastics

Plastics

A scanning electron micrograph of the surface of a sheet of biodegradable plastic, plastic that is able to be decomposed (broken into smaller parts) by bacteria. This spherical object is one of many granules of starch embedded in the surface of the plastic. When the plastic is buried in soil, the starch grains take up water and expand. This breaks the material into small fragments, increasing the contact area with the soil bacteria that digest plastic. *(Reproduced by permission of Photo Researchers, Inc.)*

The term plastic can be used as both an adjective and a noun. As an adjective, the term refers to any material that can be shaped or molded, with or without the application of heat. In this respect, objects such as soft waxes, asphalt, and moist clays are said to be plastic.

As a noun, the term describes a natural or synthetic polymer. A polymer is a material whose molecules consist of very long chains of one or two repeating units known as monomers. As an example, the synthetic polymer called polyethylene consists of thousands of ethylene units joined to each other in long chains. If the letter E is taken to represent an ethylene unit (monomer), then the polymer polyethylene can be represented as:

-E-E-E-E-E-E-E-E-E-E-E-E-E-E-E-E-E-E-E-E-E-E-E-E-E-E-E-E-E-E-E-E-E-

Although the term plastic is strictly defined as either a natural or synthetic material, it is probably understood by most people today to re-

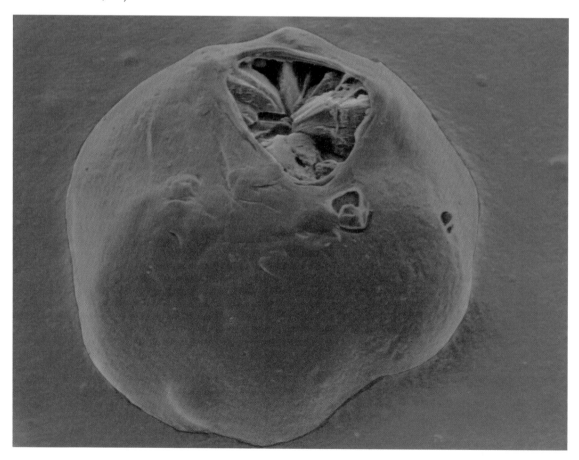

Words to Know

Composite: A combination of a plastic and one or more additives that has special properties not possessed by the plastic alone.

Monomer: A fundamental unit of which a polymer is composed.

Polymer: A substance composed of very large molecular chains that consist of repeating structural units known as monomers.

Thermoplastic: A polymer that softens when heated and that returns to its original condition when cooled to ordinary temperatures.

Thermosetting plastic (or thermoset): A polymer that solidifies when heated and that cannot be melted a second time.

fer primarily to artificial materials. Substances such as nylon, Styrofoam™, Plexiglass™, Teflon™, and polyvinyl chloride (PVC) are examples of such materials.

Thermoplastic and thermosetting plastics

Plastics can be subdivided into two large categories: thermoplastic and thermosetting. The former term refers to a material that can be melted and shaped over and over again. Examples of thermoplastics include acetal, acrylic, cellulose acetate, polyethylene, polystyrene, vinyl, and nylon.

A thermosetting plastic, in contrast, can be melted and shaped only once. If it is then heated a second time, it tends to crack or disintegrate. Examples of thermosetting plastics (or just thermosets) include amino, epoxy, and phenolic and unsaturated polyesters.

Additives

Very few plastics are used in their pure state. Many different materials known as additives are added to improve their properties. Products consisting of pure plastics and additives are known as composites. For example, the strength of a plastic can be increased by adding glass, carbon, boron, or metal fibers to it. Materials known as plasticizers make the plastics more pliable and easier to work with. Some typical plasticizers include low-melting solids, organic liquids, camphor, and castor oil. Fillers are materials made of small particles that make a plastic more resistant to fire; attack by heat, light, or chemicals; and abrasion. They also can be used to add color to the plastic.

[*See also* **Polymer**]

Plate tectonics

Plate tectonics is the geologic theory that Earth's crust is made up of rigid plates that "float" on the surface of the planet. Tectonics comes from the Greek word meaning "builder." The movement of the plates toward or away from each other either directly or indirectly creates the major geologic features at Earth's surface.

Plate tectonics revolutionized the way geologists view Earth. Like the theory of evolution in biology, plate tectonics is the unifying concept of geology. It explains nearly all of Earth's major surface features and activities. These include faults and earthquakes, volcanoes and volcanism, mountains and mountain building, and even the origin of the continents and ocean basins.

Continental drift

Plate tectonics is a comparatively new idea. The theory of plate tectonics gained widespread acceptance only in the 1960s. About 50 years earlier, German geophysicist Alfred Wegener (1880–1930) developed a related theory known as continental drift. Wegener contended that the positions of Earth's continents are not fixed. He believed instead that they are mobile and over time drift about on Earth's surface—hence the name continental drift.

Wegener's most obvious evidence for his theory was the fact that several of the world's continents fit together like pieces in a jig-saw puzzle. Based on this, he proposed that the continents of the world were previously joined together in one large continental mass, a supercontinent he called Pangaea (pronounced pan-JEE-ah). Wegener believed that this supercontinent had subsequently broken up into the six present-day continents. However, Wegener could not provide a convincing explanation as to what moved the continents around the surface of the planet. That answer came with the theory of plate tectonics.

Plate structure

Earth's tectonic plates are rigid slabs of rock. Geologists divide the interior of Earth into layers, based on their composition (from solid to liq-

Words to Know

Asthenosphere: Portion of the mantle beneath the lithosphere composed of partially melted material.

Convection current: Circular movement of a fluid in response to alternating heating and cooling.

Convergence: The movement of two plates toward one another.

Crust: Thin, solid outer portion of Earth.

Divergence: Separation of two plates as they move in opposing directions.

Lithosphere: Rigid uppermost section of the mantle combined with the crust.

Mantle: Thick, dense layer of rock that underlies Earth's crust.

Ocean trench: Deep depression in the seafloor, created by an oceanic plate being forced downward into the subsurface by another, overriding plate.

Plate margin: The boundaries where plates meet.

Plates: Large regions of Earth's surface, composed of the crust and uppermost mantle, which move about, forming many of Earth's major geologic surface features.

Seafloor spreading: Process in which new seafloor forms as molten rock from Earth's interior rises toward the surface, pushing the existing seafloor out of its way.

Subduction: Tectonic process that involves one plate being forced down into the mantle at an oceanic trench, where it eventually undergoes partial melting.

Transform motion: Horizontal plate movement in which one plate slides past another.

uid). The thin outer portion of the planet is the crust. Beneath that is the mantle, which is solid near the top and "soft" or partially melted beginning at a depth of about 40 miles (65 kilometers) beneath the surface. The crust and the rigid portion of the mantle compose the lithosphere. The soft portion of the mantle is called the asthenosphere.

It is the lithosphere that is broken up into plates, which move about while floating upon the underlying asthenosphere. There are about eight major plates and several smaller ones that are in constant contact with each other. When one plate moves, it causes other plates to move. These plates have many different shapes and sizes. Some, such as the Juan de Fuca plate off the west coast of Washington State, have surface areas of a few thousand square miles. The largest, the Pacific plate, underlies most of the Pacific Ocean and covers an area of hundreds of thousands of square miles.

Plate movement

Most modern geologists believe convection currents in the asthenosphere are the driving force for plate motion. The heat energy at the center of the planet is carried to the surface by currents. As they reach the surface, the currents cool and begin to sink back toward the center. Below the crust, pressure exerted on the bottom of the plates by the convection currents helps to push the plates along. Plates move at rates of

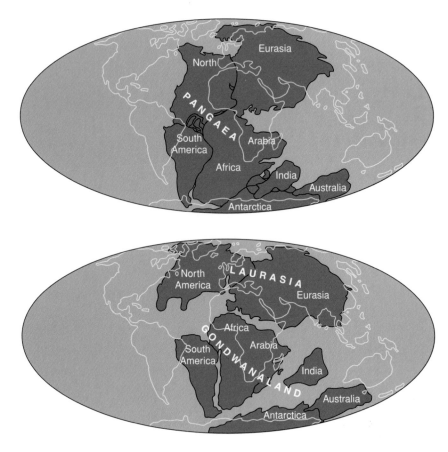

The Pangaea supercontinent (top) and after it is broken up into Laurasia and Gondwanaland (bottom). Contemporary continental outlines are shown in gray. *(Reproduced by permission of The Gale Group.)*

about 1 inch (2.5 centimeters) per year. The fastest plates move more than 4 inches (10 centimeters) per year.

Plate interactions

Tectonic plates can interact in one of three ways. They can move toward one another, or converge. They can move away from one another, or diverge. Or they can slide past one another, or transform. The boundaries where plates meet are known as plate margins. The types of geologic activity that occur when two plates interact is dependent on the nature of the plate interaction and of the margins. Plate margins come in three varieties: oceanic-oceanic, continental-continental, and continental-oceanic.

Oceanic-oceanic plates. When two oceanic plates converge, one of the plates subducts or sinks underneath the other, forming a deep depression called an ocean trench. The subducted plate sinks downward into the mantle where it begins to melt. Molten rock from the melting plate rises toward the surface and forms a chain of volcanic islands, or a volcanic island arc, behind the ocean trench. When oceanic plates diverge, a ridge (mountain chain) develops and seafloor spreading occurs. Molten rock pushes up at the divergent margin, creating mountains and an expanding seafloor. Today, Europe and North America move about 3 inches (7.5 centimeters) farther apart every year as the Atlantic Ocean grows wider.

Continental-continental plates. Continental-continental convergent plates act quite differently than oceanic-oceanic plates. Continental crust is too light to be carried downward into a trench. At continental-continental convergent margins neither plate subducts. The two continental plates converge, buckle, and compress to form complex mountains ranges of great height. Convergence of this sort produced the Himalayas when the Indian-Australian plate collided with the Eurasian plate.

Continental-continental divergence causes a continent to separate into two or more smaller continents when it is ripped apart along a series of fractures. The forces of divergence literally tear a continent apart as the two or more blocks of continental crust begin slowly moving apart and magma pushes into the rift formed between them. Eventually, if the process of continental rifting continues, a new sea is born between the two continents. Rifting between the Arabian and African plates formed the Red Sea in this way.

Continental-oceanic plates. When continental and oceanic plates converge, the oceanic plate (which is denser) subducts below the edge of the continental plate. Volcanoes form as result, but in this setting, the chain of volcanoes forms on the continental crust. This volcanic mountain chain, known as a volcanic arc, is usually several hundred miles in-

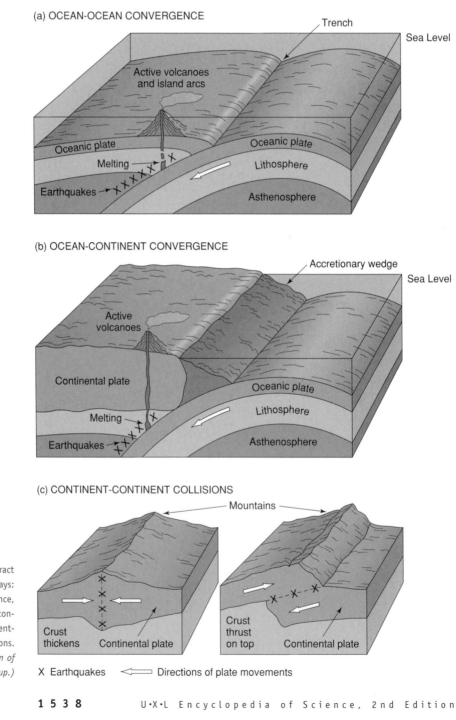

(a) OCEAN-OCEAN CONVERGENCE

Trench

Sea Level

Active volcanoes and island arcs

Oceanic plate

Melting

Earthquakes

Oceanic plate

Lithosphere

Asthenosphere

(b) OCEAN-CONTINENT CONVERGENCE

Accretionary wedge

Sea Level

Active volcanoes

Continental plate

Melting

Earthquakes

Oceanic plate

Lithosphere

Asthenosphere

(c) CONTINENT-CONTINENT COLLISIONS

Mountains

Crust thickens   Continental plate

Crust thrust on top   Continental plate

X Earthquakes   ⟸ Directions of plate movements

Tectonic plates can interact in one of three ways: a) ocean-ocean convergence, b) ocean-continental convergence, or c) continent-continent collisions. *(Reproduced by permission of The Gale Group.)*

land from the plate margin. The Andes Mountains of South America and the Cascade Mountains of North America are examples of volcanic arcs. No continental-oceanic divergent margins exist today. They are unlikely to form and would quickly become oceanic-oceanic divergent margins as seafloor spreading occurred.

Transform motion. In addition to convergence and divergence, transform motion may occur along plate margins. Transform margins are less spectacular than convergent and divergent ones, and the type of plates involved is really of no significance. As two rock plates slide past one another at a margin, a crack or fault develops. The energy generated by the movement is often released in the form of an earthquake. The best known example of a transform plate margin is the San Andreas Fault in California, where the Pacific and North American plates are in contact.

[*See also* **Earthquake; Earth's interior; Fault; Geologic map; Ocean; Volcano**]

Pluto

Pluto, the ninth and farthest planet from the Sun, is one of the least well understood objects in the solar system. It is the smallest of the major planets and has a most unusual orbit. Pluto is only 1,428 miles (2,300 kilometers) in diameter. Since the planet is 3.66 billion miles (5.89 billion kilometers) away from the Sun, it takes almost 250 years for it to complete one revolution around the Sun. However, it takes Pluto only 6.39 Earth days to complete one rotation about its own axis.

In Greek mythology, Pluto is the god of the underworld. The planet was given its name for several reason. First, due to its great distance from the Sun, Pluto is almost always dark. The sunlight it receives is about equal in intensity to moonlight on Earth. Second, Pluto is the mythological brother of Jupiter and Neptune. And finally, the planet's name begins with "PL," the initials of Percival Lowell (1855–1916), the American astronomer who spent the final years of his life searching for the elusive planet.

The search for Pluto

Shortly after the discovery of Neptune in 1846, astronomers began looking for an even more distant planet. They believed some celestial body existed at the outer reaches of the solar system that caused disturbances in the orbit of Uranus. The gravitational field of Neptune accounted for some of its neighbor's orbital irregularities, but not all of them.

Percival Lowell used traditional mathematical calculations to guess the location of the suspected planet. He also set up a photographic search for it, but all his attempts proved unsuccessful. Pluto was finally discovered in 1930 during a painstaking search of photographic plates by American astronomer Clyde Tombaugh while he was working at the Lowell Observatory in Arizona.

The properties of Pluto

Before Pluto was located, astronomers had expected it to be a large planet about the size of Jupiter, since it was able to influence the orbit of Uranus, located two planets away. At that time, the solar system appeared to fit a neat pattern: small, dense planets were closest to the Sun and giant, gaseous planets were farther away. Pluto broke this pattern: it is a small, dense planet at the farthest reaches from the Sun.

Pluto's orbit also differs from the pattern set by the other planets in the solar system. While the other eight planets orbit the Sun on the same plane, Pluto travels on an inclined orbit that crosses that plane. Its orbit—the most oval in shape of all the planets—lies mostly outside of that of its closest neighbor, Neptune. At times, however, it crosses inside Neptune's orbit, bringing it closer to the Sun than Neptune.

Pluto is so distant that no Earth-bound telescope has been able to provide a detailed picture of its surface features. The best image to date was taken by the Hubble Space Telescope (HST) in early 1996, in which the planet looks like a fuzzy soccer ball. The HST only revealed that Pluto has frozen gases, icy polar caps, and mysterious bright and dark spots.

Beyond that, astronomers can rely only on imprecise observations and what is known about the planet's density to paint a more complete picture of the planet. Pluto is probably composed of mostly rock and some ice, with surface temperatures between -350 and $-380°F$ (-212 and $-228°C$). The bright areas on its surface are most likely nitrogen ice, solid methane, and carbon monoxide. The dark spots may hold some form of organic material, possible hydrocarbons from the chemical splitting and freezing of methane.

Pluto's atmosphere is probably made of nitrogen, carbon monoxide, and methane. At Pluto's perihelion (pronounced pear-a-HEE-lee-an; the point on its orbit closest to the Sun), its atmosphere exists in a gaseous state. For most of its orbit, the atmosphere is frozen.

Its only moon

Much of what is known about Pluto was learned following the 1978 discovery of Pluto's moon, Charon (pronounced Karen, and named for the mythological character who transported the dead to the underworld). Prior to Charon's discovery, astronomers thought Pluto and its moon together were one larger object. Charon has a diameter over half that of Pluto, making it the largest moon relative to its planet in the solar system. For this reason, some astronomers consider the two bodies to be a double planet.

An artist's view of Pluto and its only moon, Charon. *(Reproduced by permission of National Aeronautics and Space Administration.)*

The origin of Pluto

Most theories regarding Pluto's origin connect the planet with Neptune's moon Triton. This is because Pluto, like Triton, rotates in a direction opposite that of most other planets and their satellites.

One theory is that Pluto used to be one of Neptune's moons. Struck by a massive object, Pluto was broken in two, creating Charon. The two were then sent into orbit around the Sun. A more popular theory, however, is that both Pluto and Triton started out in independent orbits and that Triton was captured by Neptune's gravitational field.

Trips to Pluto

More questions about Pluto and Charon were to be answered early in the twenty-first century when the National Aeronautics and Space Administration (NASA) planned to send the first unmanned mission to Pluto and its moon. The *Pluto-Kuiper Express,* which was scheduled to be launched in 2004, was to have consisted of two spacecraft. They were to arrive at Pluto by 2012. They were expected to encounter Pluto near its perihelion, before its atmosphere froze once again, a seasonal deep freeze that lasts more than 100 years. The spacecraft were to study the atmosphere, surface features, and geologic composition of Pluto and Charon, then fly by Pluto into the Kuiper Disk, a ring filled with hundreds of thousands of small, icy objects that are well-preserved remnants of the early solar system. This ring is located between Neptune and Pluto (sometimes beyond Pluto, depending on its oval orbit), some 3.6 billion miles (5.8 billion kilometers) from Earth.

In September 2000, however, NASA issued a stop-work order on the project because of spiraling costs. The project was then canceled in April 2001 when the 2002 budget issued by President George W. Bush's administration provided no money for it.

[*See also* **Solar system**]

Poisons and toxins

A poison is any chemical that kills or injures an organism. The term toxin refers to a poison produced by a living organism, such as a microorganism, a plant, or an animal. In everyday practice, the terms poison and toxin are often used interchangeably.

Words to Know

Acute toxicity: A poisonous effect produced by a single, short-term exposure to a toxic chemical, resulting in obvious health effects and even death of the organism.

Chronic toxicity: A poisonous effect that is produced by a long period of exposure to a moderate, less-than-acute dose of some toxic chemical.

Exposure: The concentration of a chemical in the environment or the accumulated dose that an organism encounters.

LD_{50}: The amount of a chemical required to kill one-half of a population of organisms in a short period of time.

It is important to understand that any chemical is potentially poisonous. All that is required for a chemical to cause toxicity is a dose large enough to cause some harmful effect. For example, water could be considered toxic if a person drank four gallons of it all at once. In such a case, the water would cause serious bodily harm—even death. In a large quantity, then, water could be classified as a poison.

Toxicity

The term toxicity is used to express how poisonous a chemical is. Scientists distinguish between two kinds of toxicity: acute and chronic. Acute toxicity refers to the amount of damage caused by a chemical after a short-term exposure to a large dose of the chemical. For example, a person might accidentally swallow a tablespoon of rat poison. The effects caused by that accident would be described as the chemical's acute toxicity.

Scientists have various ways of measuring the acute toxicity of a chemical. Perhaps the most common is called LD_{50}. The abbreviation LD_{50} stands for "lethal dose, 50 percent." It is the amount of the chemical required to kill one-half of a population of organisms in a short period of time.

Some chemicals cause effects that are difficult to observe over a short period of time. These effects are referred to as chronic toxicity. For example, a person who works with the mineral asbestos runs the risk of developing various respiratory disorders late in his or her life. Such disorders include emphysema, chronic bronchitis, and lung cancer. These

LD$_{50}$ Value for Various Chemicals

Chemical	LD$_{50}$ Value*
TCDD (a form of dioxin)	0.01
Tetrodotoxin (globefish toxin)	0.01
Saxitoxin (shellfish poison)	0.8
Carbofuran (a pesticide)	10
Phosphamidon (an insecticide)	24
Nicotine	50
Caffeine	200
DDT (an insecticide)	200
2,4-D (an herbicide)	370
Mirex (an insecticide)	740
Acetylsalicylic acid (aspirin)	1,700
Malathion (an insecticide)	2,000
Sodium chloride (table salt)	3,750
Glyphosate (an herbicide)	4,300
Ethanol (drinking alcohol)	13,700
Sucrose (table sugar)	30,000

* In milligrams of chemical per kilogram of body weight.

disorders may not show up for many years after exposure to asbestos. Thus, they are known as chronic effects of exposure to a poison.

In humans and other animals, long-term chronic toxicity can occur in the form of increased rates of birth defects, cancer, organ damage, and reproductive problems, such as spontaneous abortions. In plants, chronic toxicity can often be recognized in terms of decreased productivity (in comparison with plants that are not chronically exposed to the toxic chemicals in question). Because they develop over very long periods of time and are often difficult to recognize in their early stages, chronic toxicities are much more difficult to detect than are acute toxicities.

For every poison, there is a certain threshold of tolerance below which no harmful effect is likely to occur. For example, the threshold for a particular chemical might be 5 milligrams of the chemical per kilogram of body weight. If a person is exposed to less than 5 milligrams of the chemical per kilogram of body weight, no harmful effect is likely to occur. If the exposure exceeds that amount, then the symptoms of poisoning begin to appear.

Some naturally occurring poisons

Many poisonous chemicals are present naturally in the environment. For example, naturally occurring elements such as arsenic, mercury, lead, and cadmium are toxic in various concentrations to both plants and animals. Areas where these elements occur in large concentrations are usually barren of plants and animals.

Other naturally occurring toxins are substances produced by plants and animals. In many cases, these toxins are part of a plant or animal's natural defense system, protecting them from other plants and animals that prey on them. One such example is the chemical tetrodotoxin, synthesized by the Japanese globefish (*Spheroides rubripes*). Tetrodotoxin is extremely toxic even if ingested in tiny amounts. Only slightly less toxic is saxitoxin, synthesized by species of marine phytoplankton but accumulated by shellfish. When people eat these shellfish, a deadly syndrome known as paralytic shellfish poisoning results. There are numerous other

Venom dripping from the fangs of a snake in Brazil. *(Reproduced by permission of World Health Forum.)*

examples of deadly biochemicals such as snake and bee venoms, toxins produced by disease-causing microorganisms, and mushroom poisons.

Poisons produced by human technology

In the modern world, humans are responsible for many of the toxic chemicals that are now being dispersed into the environment. In some cases, human actions cause toxic damage by emitting large quantities of chemicals that also occur naturally, such as sulfur dioxide, hydrocarbons, and metals. Release of these chemicals as the result of human activities only increases the severity of problems that may already exist because of the natural presence of these chemicals.

Humans, however, also produce and release to the environment large quantities of chemicals that do not occur naturally. These synthetic (made in a lab) chemicals include thousands of different pesticides, medicines, and various kinds of industrial chemicals, all of them occurring in complex mixtures of various forms. Many of these chemicals affect humans and other organisms directly, as is the case with many pesticides. In other cases, toxicity occurs indirectly. An example is the class of compounds known as the chlorofluorocarbons (CFCs). Normally these chemicals are quite inert (inactive). However, when they find their way to the upper atmosphere, they break apart into simpler chemicals that consume ozone, the gas that protects life on Earth from harmful ultraviolet radiation. As a result, the risk of disorders such as skin cancers, cataracts, and immune disorders greatly increases.

In an attempt to control the effect of highly toxic chemicals, 122 nations met in late 2000 and agreed to a treaty calling for the global elimination of 12 chemical pollutants. Environmentalists have called these the "dirty dozen." The twelve include eight pesticides (aldrin, chlordane, DDT, dieldrin, endrin, heptachlor, mirex, and toxaphene), two types of industrial chemicals (hexachlorobenzene and polychlorinated biphenyls or PCBs), and two types of industrial byproducts (dioxins and furans). These toxic pollutants were chosen not because they are the most dangerous, but because they are the most widely studied. The treaty must be ratified by 50 nations before it can take effect.

[*See also* **Ozone; Pollution control**]

Poliomyelitis

Poliomyelitis, or polio, is a serious infectious disease that attacks muscle-controlling nerves and can eventually cause paralysis. Poliomyelitis, some-

Words to Know

Epidemic: Rapidly spreading outbreak of a contagious disease.

Iron lung: Device developed in 1928 by Philip Drinker to maintain artificial respiration in a person over a long period of time.

Sabin vaccine: Oral polio vaccine developed by Albert Sabin from weakened live polio viruses and introduced in 1961.

Salk vaccine: Polio vaccine developed by Jonas Salk in the mid-1950s from dead polio viruses and given through injection.

times called infantile paralysis, is caused by one of three related viruses, and it primarily affects children. However, adults can also be infected. There is no drug that can cure the disease once a person has been infected.

Poliomyelitis is infectious, meaning it is spread primarily through contact with someone who already has the disease. The virus enters the body through the mouth and then enters the bloodstream. Once in the central nervous system, it travels along nerve pathways. In severe cases, it reaches the spinal cord or the brain where it causes lesions (abnormal changes in the structure of body tissue).

Symptoms usually begin to show one to three weeks after the virus is contracted. In some cases, the attack may be so mild that it goes unnoticed. The body quickly develops immunity and the virus is eliminated. A more severe attack gives rise to symptoms that resemble those of influenza (fever, sore throat, vomiting, diarrhea, stiff neck and back, and muscle pain). About two-thirds of people infected in such a way recover without suffering any paralysis.

A serious attack occurs if the virus reaches the central nervous system. Muscle tissue weakens and paralysis develops. Usually the paralysis is only temporary, and about 50 percent of people infected recover without permanent disability. However, if any of the cells attacked by the virus are destroyed, they cannot be replaced and muscle function is permanently impaired. About 25 percent of people who recover after being seriously infected have severe permanent disability.

If the nerve cells of the brain are attacked (a condition known as bulbar poliomyelitis), the muscles controlling swallowing, heartbeat, and breathing are paralyzed. The result is death.

Development of the iron lung

Incidents of poliomyelitis can be traced back to ancient Egypt. The first recorded poliomyelitis epidemic (a rapidly spreading outbreak of a contagious disease) was in Sweden in 1881. From that time until the mid-1900s, there were regular epidemics throughout the world.

To help those people infected with poliomyelitis whose respiratory (breathing) muscles had been paralyzed, American physiologist Philip Drinker (1893–1977) invented the Drinker tank respirator (commonly known as the iron lung) in 1928. It is a device to maintain artificial respiration in a person over a long period of time. The iron lung is an airtight cylindrical steel drum that encloses the entire body, with only a patient's head exposed. Pumps connected to the device lower and raise air pressure within the drum, which contracts and expands a patient's chest walls (imitating the action of breathing). Many poliomyelitis patients were kept alive in such a manner, but it was not a cure for the disease.

Salk and Sabin vaccines

In the early 1950s, American microbiologist Jonas Salk (1914–1995) developed the first vaccine to prevent the spread of the disease. The Salk vaccine is composed of killed poliomyelitis virus. A series of three of

Polio victims kept alive by iron lungs. *(Reproduced by permission of the Corbis Corporation [Bellevue].)*

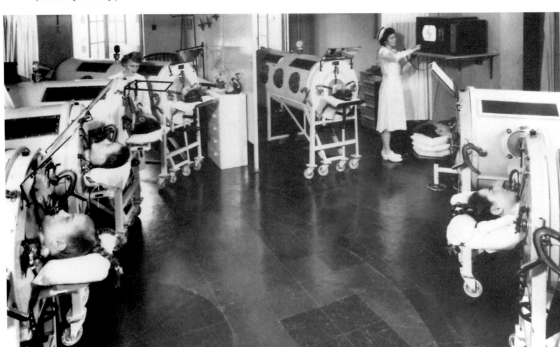

four injections with the killed-virus vaccine prompts the body's immune system to produce antibodies that will attack any future invading forms of the disease. In 1955, the vaccine was officially pronounced effective, potent, and safe in almost 90 percent of cases. The major defense the Salk vaccine provides against polio viruses is to prevent them from spreading from the digestive system to the nervous and respiratory systems. But it cannot prevent the viruses from entering the intestinal tract.

In the late 1950s, Russian-born American virologist Albert Sabin (1906–1993) developed a vaccine that has proven to provide longer immunity against the disease than the Salk vaccine. The Sabin vaccine is composed of live (but weakened and harmless) poliomyelitis virus. After four years of worldwide tests, the vaccine became available to the public in 1961. The advantage of the Sabin vaccine is that it is given orally and offers protection with only a single dose. The vaccine goes straight to the intestinal tract and builds up immunity there as well as in other parts of the body.

Both vaccines are effective against all forms of the poliomyelitis virus. Near the end of the twentieth century, health organizations reported that poliomyelitis was close to extinction in the Western Hemisphere.

[*See also* **Vaccine**]

Pollution

Pollution refers to situations in which some material or some form of energy occurs in larger quantity than can be tolerated by humans, plants, or animals without suffering some kind of harm. Probably the best-known forms of pollution are air and water pollution, which are discussed below. But other forms of pollution also exist. For example, the term noise pollution has been used to describe the loud noise level of airplane takeoffs and landings, construction, highway traffic, boom boxes, and other modern-day machines. Similarly, the expression visual pollution has been used to describe areas so clogged with signs, billboards, and other objects that the beauty of the natural environment is diminished.

Natural and anthropogenic pollution

Pollution can be caused both by natural sources and humans. Volcanic eruptions are an example of natural sources of pollution. When a volcano explodes, it releases sulfur dioxide, carbon monoxide, solid particles, and other materials into the air at a much greater rate than is

Words to Know

Acid: Substances that when dissolved in water are capable of reacting with a base to form salts and release hydrogen ions.

Acid rain: A form of precipitation that is significantly more acidic than neutral water, often produced as the result of industrial processes.

Anthropogenic: Any effect caused by humans.

Fossil fuel: Fuels formed by decaying plants and animals on the ocean floors that were covered by layers of sand and mud. Over millions of years, the layers of sediment created pressure and heat that helped bacteria change the decaying organic material into oil and gas.

Greenhouse effect: The warming of Earth's atmosphere as the result of the capture of heat by carbon dioxide molecules in the air.

Oxide: An inorganic compound whose only negative part is the element oxygen.

Oxygen-demanding agent: Any substance that reacts with oxygen dissolved in water.

normally the case. Plants, animals, and humans may be killed or injured by these materials.

A concrete example of natural pollution can be found at an area known as the Smoking Hills, located in a remote wilderness in the Canadian Arctic. The local environment around Smoking Hills is virtually uninfluenced by humans. However, naturally occurring low-grade coal deposits found in the area have spontaneously ignited from time to time, causing the release of clouds of sulfur dioxide over the nearby tundra.

As this gas is carried to Earth's surface, soil and freshwater become acidified. At some level, this acidification causes metals to become soluble (able to be dissolved). The toxicity (poisons) associated with sulfur dioxide, acidity, and soluble metals at the Smoking Hills has caused great damage to the structure and function of the local ecosystem.

History of anthropogenic pollution

Natural forms of pollution have existed since the dawn of time, and there is not much humans can do to control such events. On the other hand,

Particulate: Solid matter in the form of tiny particles in the atmosphere.

Primary pollutant: Any pollutant released directly from a source to the atmosphere.

Radiation: Energy transmitted in the form of electromagnetic waves or subatomic particles.

Secondary pollutant: Any pollutant formed in the atmosphere from compounds released from some source.

Smog: A form of air pollution characterized by hazy skies and a tendency to cause respiratory problems among humans.

Thermal inversion: A condition in which there is an atmospheric zone in which temperature increases with altitude, instead of the usual decrease with increasing altitude.

Volatile organic compound: Any organic liquid that changes easily (volatilizes) to a gas.

the vast majority of pollution affecting human societies today originates from human activities and is therefore susceptible to human control.

Human-caused pollution is sometimes referred to as anthropogenic pollution. Anthropogenic pollution has existed for centuries. People living in London, England, in the late eighteenth century, for example, were exposed to huge quantities of noxious gases in the air and dangerous levels of harmful materials in their water supplies. However, most people of the time probably accepted such risks as part of being a city dweller.

Modern concerns about pollution began to increase in the 1960s largely as the result of two factors. First, population growth in many urban areas meant that more people and more industries were releasing a higher concentration of pollutants to the environment than ever before. Second, modern science had developed a number of new materials and new procedures that resulted in the release of many new and often dangerous chemicals to the environment.

As people became more and more conscious of pollution problems, they began calling for government efforts to control the release of pollutants and to clean up a dirty environment. Some results of this effort included the Clean Air Acts of 1965, 1970, and 1977; the Safe Drinking Water Act of 1974; the Clean Water Act of 1977; and the Toxic Substances Control Act of 1976.

Air pollution

A complete list of air pollutants would include nearly two dozen solids, liquids, and gases. It would include well-known pollutants such as sulfur oxides and carbon monoxide and less-familiar materials such as pesticides and fluorides. In terms of the quantities of pollutants released in a year, the five materials that cause the most damage are sulfur oxides, oxides of nitrogen, carbon monoxide, particulate matter, and volatile organic compounds.

Sulfur oxides, oxides of nitrogen, and carbon monoxide are chemical compounds. Particulate matter and volatile organic compounds are groups of related pollutants. The term particulate refers to tiny specks of solid matter in the atmosphere, including smoke, haze, aerosols, and tiny particles of carbon. Volatile organic compounds are organic liquids, such as benzene, toluene, the xylenes, and trichloromethane, that change easily (volatilize) to a gas.

Effects of air pollutants. By definition, all forms of air pollution have some harmful effect on humans, other animals, plants, or other materials in the environment. For example, carbon monoxide is a well-known toxic gas that reduces the blood's ability to transport oxygen. Prolonged exposure to carbon monoxide can cause heart and respiratory disorders; headaches, nausea, and fatigue; and, at high enough concentrations, coma and death. The oxides of both sulfur and nitrogen attack the human respiratory system, leading to irritated eyes and throat and impaired breathing (at low concentrations), and to emphysema, bronchitis, and lung cancer (at higher concentrations).

The effects of particulate matter are wide, from preventing photosynthesis (food production) in plants to clogging the breathing passages in lungs (leading to respiratory disorders). Particulate matter also soils buildings, statutes, and other objects, leading to their decay and deterioration.

Sources of air pollution. The major single source of air pollutants is the combustion (burning) of fossil fuels (coal, oil, and gas) to run industrial machines and generate electricity. All anthropogenic pollutants can be traced to some extent to this source. A second major source of pollutants is the incomplete combustion of fuel in cars, trucks, railroad trains, airplanes, and other forms of transportation. Smaller amounts of pollutants are released during the incineration of solid wastes and by a variety of industrial processes.

In some cases, pollutants are released by these sources directly to the air and are known, therefore, as primary pollutants. Sulfur dioxide, oxides of nitrogen, and carbon monoxide are all primary pollutants. In other cases, materials released by a source undergo a chemical reaction in the atmosphere and are converted to a secondary pollutant. Examples of secondary pollutants are ozone and peroxyacyl nitrates (PANs), major components of the form of air pollution known as smog.

Specialized forms of air pollution. Under specialized conditions, certain forms of air pollution have developed that are so dramatic or so serious that they have been given special names. These conditions include smog, acid rain, the greenhouse effect, and ozone depletion.

The term smog actually applies to two quite different atmospheric conditions. The term itself comes from a combination of the words smoke and fog. One form of smog, known as industrial smog, is produced when sulfur dioxide, particulates, and other pollutants released by industrial and household burning of fossil fuels is trapped by a thermal inversion. A thermal inversion is an atmospheric condition in which a layer of cold air is trapped by a layer of warm air above it. Some of the most dramatic photographs of urban areas covered by air pollution are those that show a city smothered in a cloud of smog.

A second form of smog is photochemical smog, produced when oxides of nitrogen, produced largely by internal-combustion engines (those most often used in automobiles, for example), react with oxygen in the air to form a complex mixture of pollutants that includes ozone, PANs, and other organic compounds. Photochemical smog often has a similar appearance and similar effects to those of industrial smog. Indeed, in most cities, the two forms of smog occur in combination with each other.

Acid rain. Acid rain, or more generally acid precipitation, is the name given to any form of precipitation (rain, snow, sleet, hail, fog) that is more acidic than normal. The high acidity of acid precipitation results from the formation of acids in the atmosphere from chemicals released by human sources.

Most powerplants that produce electricity release as by-products large quantities of nitrogen and sulfur oxides. Once in the atmosphere, these oxides react with moisture in the air to produce nitric and sulfuric acid. When precipitation occurs, these acids are carried to Earth's surface, where they attack plants, animals, and nonliving materials. Some experts believe that large regions of forests on the east coast of the United States and Canada have been badly damaged by acid precipitation resulting from gases released by industrial plants in the midwestern United States. Acid precipitation has also been blamed for the death of fish and other aquatic organisms and for damage to stone buildings and sculptures.

Greenhouse effect. Carbon dioxide is normally not considered to be a pollutant since it has no harmful effects on plants or animals. It does have one other effect, however, that may affect life on Earth. Solar energy that reaches Earth's atmosphere experiences a variety of fates. Some of that energy is reflected back into space, while some passes through the atmosphere and reaches Earth. Of the solar energy that reaches Earth's surface, some is absorbed and some is reflected back into the atmosphere. A large fraction of the reflected energy is captured by carbon dioxide molecules in the air and retained as heat. This effect has been compared to the way in which the glass in a greenhouse may capture heat and is called, therefore, the greenhouse effect. Experts believe that, without the greenhouse effect, Earth's temperature would be about 8°C (18°F) cooler than it actually is, making it impossible for most forms of life to survive.

Since the turn of the twentieth century, however, the rate at which carbon dioxide is being added to Earth's atmosphere has increased dra-

Pollution from auto emissions and industry can come together to form smog, a foggy, pollutant-filled haze, as in Long Beach, California. *(Reproduced by permission of Greenpeace Photos.)*

matically. The combustion of fossil fuels for heating, industrial operations, transportation, and other uses is primarily responsible for this trend. With the increase in carbon dioxide in the atmosphere comes an increased greenhouse effect and, some experts believe, a general warming of the planet's annual average temperature. In a report released in early 2001, scientists concluded that if greenhouse emissions are not curtailed, the average global surface temperature could rise by nearly 11°F (6°C) over the next 100 years. The scientists also stated that man-made pollution has "contributed substantially" to global warming and that Earth is likely to get a lot hotter than previously predicted. Such a warming could cause a massive melting of the polar ice caps, resulting in the flooding of many coastal areas.

Ozone depletion. Ozone is a form of oxygen whose molecules contain three atoms (O_3) rather than two atoms (O_2). Ozone occurs in very small concentrations in upper regions of Earth's atmosphere, where it has a function vital to life on Earth. Ozone molecules have the ability to capture infrared radiation that enters Earth's atmosphere as part of sunlight. Infrared radiation is known to have a number of undesirable effects on plants and animals, from damage to leaves and fruits of plants to skin cancer and eye problems in humans.

Scientists have learned that certain synthetic (human-made) chemicals known as the chlorofluorocarbons (CFCs) have the ability to attack and destroy ozone molecules in the atmosphere. CFC molecules are broken apart by solar energy with the release of chlorine atoms. These chlorine atoms then attack ozone molecules and convert them to ordinary oxygen.

The loss of ozone molecules as the result of attacks by CFCs means that the ozone "shield" in the atmosphere is decreasing in concentration. With this decrease, a larger percentage of ultraviolet radiation is likely to reach Earth's surface, resulting in an increase in complications from exposure to ultraviolet radiation.

Air pollution controls. A number of approaches are possible for the reduction of air pollutants. For example, it would be desirable simply to reduce the use of various processes that release pollutants into the air. Getting people to ride bicycles or walk to work instead of driving a car is a simple way of reducing the emission of nitrogen oxides and carbon monoxide.

Another approach is to convert harmful pollutants to harmless forms before they are released to the atmosphere. The catalytic convertor that is now standard equipment on passenger vehicles does just that. It converts harmful oxides of nitrogen and hydrocarbons to harmless nitrogen, oxygen, carbon dioxide, and water vapor.

Efforts can be made to trap pollutants as they are released from a source, thus preventing them from reaching the atmosphere. Devices known as scrubbers on smokestacks are an example. Polluting gases, such as oxides of sulfur and nitrogen, are captured in scrubbers, where they react with chemicals that convert them to harmless (and sometimes useful) by-products.

Water pollution

A broad variety of materials can be classified as water pollutants, including synthetic organic compounds, human and animal wastes, radioactive materials, heat, acids, sediments, and disease-causing microorganisms. The following discussion describes the major water pollutants, their sources, and possible means of control.

Oxygen-demanding agents.   An oxygen-demanding agent is some substance which, when placed into water, reacts with oxygen dissolved in the water. As oxygen is removed from the water, other organisms that also depend on that oxygen (such as fish and other forms of aquatic life) may die or migrate away from the polluted waters. Sources of food and recreation may be destroyed by the presence of such agents.

The obvious way to prevent pollution by oxygen-demanding wastes is to prevent sewage and other solid wastes from entering water supplies or to treat those wastes before they are released to lakes and rivers.

Synthetic organic chemicals.   The term synthetic organic chemical applies to a wide variety of products invented by modern chemistry to serve various human needs. These products include plastics, pesticides and herbicides, detergents, toxic by-products of industrial operations, and oils. Many of these products are directly toxic to fish, aquatic life, and even to humans. Others may not present a serious health effect to organisms, but can cause the unsightly accumulation of trash, destroying the recreational value of a waterway.

The release of synthetic organic chemicals to waterways can be controlled by establishing and enforcing methods of producing, storing, shipping, and disposing of such materials. For example, many people are accustomed simply to dumping used motor oil into city sewers. This practice guarantees that rivers and lakes will become polluted with such oils. A better practice is for cities to provide special collection procedures for used motor oils.

Industrial chemicals. A number of inorganic chemicals are released from industrial operations as the by-products of certain processes. For example, the element mercury is used in the production of light switches, air conditioners, fluorescent lights, floor waxes, medicines, plastics, paper, clothing, and photographic film, to name but a few of its applications. Each time one of these products is made, some small amount of mercury metal is likely to escape into the environment and, eventually, into lakes and rivers. This is problematic because mercury is highly toxic to humans and other organisms. It causes damage to the nervous system, kidneys, liver, and brain.

One way to limit the release of industrial chemicals to water supplies is to find alternative chemicals to use in manufacturing operations. Another approach is to pass and enforce legislation that requires appropriate methods of storage and disposal of such chemicals.

Sediments. Sediments washed from Earth's surface also pollute water. Any time it rains, a certain amount of sand, clay, silt, and other forms of earthy material are washed away. This sediment has a number of consequences, such as the silting of harbors and reservoirs, damage to shellfish and fish, reduction in the clarity of water, and the loss of water's ability to integrate (blend) oxygen-demanding wastes.

Water pollution can take many forms. This gull was choked to death by a plastic six-pack holder. *(Reproduced courtesy of the U.S. Fish and Wildlife Service.)*

The loss of sediments during rainstorms is a natural event and cannot, therefore, be totally eliminated. However, careless building and forestry practices may contribute enormously to the loss of sediments. Tree roots, for example, are important for holding soil in place. When trees are removed from an area, the soil is much more easily washed away.

Heat. Warm water is not able to dissolve as much oxygen as is cool water. If the water in a river becomes warmer, it holds less oxygen. Organisms that depend on oxygen for their survival, then, will either die or migrate to other areas. Many industrial and energy-generating plants use water in their operation. They take water from a river or lake, use it, and return it to the same body of water, but at a higher temperature. This practice, sometimes known as thermal pollution, poses a serious hazard to organisms living in the water.

The most common method for avoiding thermal pollution is to cool water discharged from a plant before returning it to a body of water. Many plants now have large cooling towers or artificial lakes through which waste waters must pass before they are returned to a lake or river.

[*See also* **Acid rain; Agrochemical; Atmosphere, composition and structure; Carbon dioxide; Carbon monoxide; DDT (dichlorodiphenyltrichloroethane); Greenhouse effect; Oil spills; Ozone**]

Pollution control

Pollution control is the process of reducing or eliminating the release of pollutants (contaminants, usually human-made) into the environment. It is regulated by various environmental agencies that establish limits for the discharge of pollutants into the air, water, and land. A wide variety of devices and systems have been developed to control air and water pollution and solid wastes.

Air pollution control

Methods of air pollution control can be divided into two categories: the control of particulate (pronounced par-TIK-you-let) emissions and the control of gaseous emissions. The term particulate refers to tiny particles of matter such as smoke, soot, and dust that are released during industrial, agricultural, or other activities. Gaseous emissions are industrial products such as sulfur dioxide, carbon monoxide, and oxides of nitrogen also released during various manufacturing operations.

Particulate control.   Methods for particulate control tend to operate on a common principle. The solid particles are separated from the gases in which they are contained by physical procedures such as passage through a settling chamber. A settling chamber is a long, wide pipe through which gases from a manufacturing process are allowed to flow. As these gases slow down in the pipe, the solid particles settle out. They can then be removed from the bottom of the pipe.

A cyclone collector is another device for removing particulates from stack gases. The gases are fed into a rotating cylindrical container.

Equipment for the complete recovery and control of acid and oxide emissions. *(Reproduced by permission of Phototake.)*

Centrifugal forces (the forces that move things away from the center of rotation) send solid particles in the gas outward against the walls of the container. They collect there briefly, then fall to the bottom of the container. Gases from which the particles have been removed then escape from the top of the container.

Gaseous emissions.　Many different methods are available for removing unwanted gases, most of which are acidic. Scrubbers are smokestack devices that contain a moist chemical such as lime, magnesium oxide, or sodium hydroxide. When gases escape from a factory and pass through a scrubber, they react with the moist chemical and are neutralized. From time to time, the scrubbers are removed from the smokestack, cleaned, and replaced.

Another method for controlling gaseous emissions is by adsorption. Activated charcoal is charcoal that has been ground into a very fine powder. In this form, charcoal has the ability to adsorb, or adhere to, other chemicals. When unwanted gases flow over activated charcoal on the inside of a smokestack, they are adsorbed on the charcoal. As with scrubbers, the charcoal is removed from time to time, and a new lining of charcoal is installed in the smokestack.

High levels of air pollution are not a necessary cost of industry, as evidenced by this cement plant in Cleveland, Ohio. *(Reproduced by permission of Greenpeace Photos.)*

Water pollution

Methods of controlling water pollution fall into three general categories: physical, chemical, and biological. For example, one form of water pollution consists of suspended solids such as fine dirt and dead organisms. These materials can be removed from water by simply allowing the water to sit quietly for a period of time, thereby allowing the pollutants to settle out, or by passing the water through a filter. (The solid pollutants are then trapped in the filter.)

Chemical reactions can be used to remove pollutants from water. For example, the addition of alum (potassium aluminum sulfate) and lime (calcium hydroxide) to water results in the formation of a thick, sticky precipitate. When the precipitate begins to settle out, it traps and carries with it solid particles, dead bacteria, and other components of polluted water.

Biological agents can also be used to remove pollutants from water. Aerobic bacteria (those that need oxygen to survive) and anaerobic bacteria (those that do not require oxygen) attack certain chemicals in polluted water and convert them to a harmless form.

Solid pollutants

Solid pollutants consist of garbage, sewage sludge, paper, plastics, and many other forms of waste materials. One method of dealing with solid pollutants is simply to bury them in dumps or landfills. Another approach is to compost them, a process in which microorganisms turn certain types of pollutants into useful fertilizers. Finally, solid pollutants can also be incinerated (burned).

Taking on pollution: a global attempt

While artificial chemicals have improved the quality of life around the world, they have also posed a threat to the health of people and wildlife. In late 2000, in an effort to control the effect of toxic global pollutants, the United Nations Environment Program organized a meeting to draft a treaty to restrict the production and use of twelve persistent organic pollutants (POPs), especially those used as pesticides. The twelve toxic chemicals cited, which environmentalists have called the "dirty dozen," include eight pesticides (aldrin, chlordane, DDT, dieldrin, endrin, heptachlor, mirex, and toxaphene), two types of industrial chemicals (hexachlorobenzene and polychlorinated biphenyls or PCBs), and two types of industrial byproducts (dioxins and furans). These toxic pollutants were chosen not because they are the most dangerous, but because they are the most widely studied. Since it is still widely used in Africa to control malaria, DDT was given a special exemption: it can be used in those countries until replacement chemicals or strategies can be developed and put into place. One hundred and twenty-two nations (including the United States) agreed to the treaty. Before it can take effect, however, at least fifty of those nations must also ratify it.

Possible future approach to cleaning up pollution

The cost of cleaning up tens of thousands of toxic sites on factory grounds, farms, and military installations is staggering. In the United States, that amount may soon exceed $700 billion. So far, the main approach has been to dig the polluting chemicals out of the ground and transport them to a landfill. However, after a decade of research, scientists in the early twenty-first century found that hundreds of species of plants, along with the fungi and bacteria that inhabit the ecosystem around their roots, seek out and often break down chemical molecules that can harm most other life. For example, there are sunflowers that capture uranium, ferns that thrive on arsenic, clovers that eat oil, and poplar trees that destroy dry-cleaning solvents. Research into using plants as pollution sponges must continue, but early reports of their helping to clean up pollution were promising.

[*See also* **Acid rain; Pollution**]

Polygon

A polygon is a geometric figure in two dimensions with three or more sides. The name comes from two Greek words, *poly,* meaning "many,"

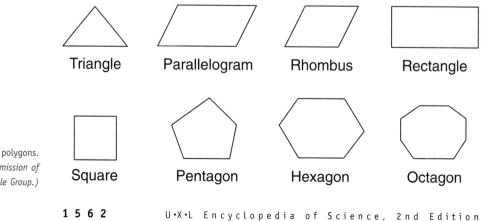

Different types of polygons.
(Reproduced by permission of The Gale Group.)

and *gon,* meaning "angle." A polygon always has as many angles as it has sides. And in general, polygons are named to indicate the number of sides or angles they contain. Thus, a hexagon has six (*hexa-* means "six") sides and six angles.

Terminology used in describing polygons

Parts and properties of polygons.

Side: Any one of the straight lines that make up the polygon.

Vertex: A point where any two of the sides of a polygon meet to form an angle.

Angle: A figure formed by the intersection of two sides.

Diagonal: A line that joins any two nonadjacent (not next to each other) vertices.

Perimeter: The sum of the length of all sides.

Area: The space enclosed within the polygon.

Types of polygons.

Equilateral: A polygon in which all sides are equal in length.

Equiangular: A polygon in which all angles are the same size.

Regular: A polygon that is both equilateral and equiangular.

Examples of polygons

The most common kinds of polygons include:

Parallelogram: A quadrilateral (four-sided figure) in which both pairs of sides are parallel and equal.

Rhombus: A parallelogram in which all four sides are equal.

Rectangle: A parallelogram in which all angles are right angles.

Square: A rectangle in which all four sides are equal.

Polymer

A polymer is a very large molecule in which one or two small units is repeated over and over again. The small repeating units are known as monomers. Imagine that a monomer can be represented by the letter A. Then a polymer made of that monomer would have the structure:

-A-A-A-A-A-A-A-A-A-A-A-A-A-A-A-A-A-A-A-A-A-A-A-A-A-A-A-

In another kind of polymer, two different monomers might be involved. If the letters A and B represent those monomers, then the polymer could be represented as:

-A-B-A-B-A-B-A-B-A-B-A-B-A-B-A-B-A-B-A-B-A-B-A-B-A-B-A-

A polymer with two different monomers is known as a copolymer.

The number of monomers (As or Bs) in a polymer is very great indeed. To accurately represent the first polymer above, for example, it might be necessary to write a few hundred or a few thousand As. We would have to fill up a page or two of this book to give an accurate formula for such a polymer.

Natural polymers

Polymers are very common in nature; some of the most widespread naturally occurring substances are polymers. Starch and cellulose are examples. Green plants have the ability to take the simple sugar known as glucose and make very long chains containing many glucose units. These long chains are molecules of starch or cellulose. If we assign the symbol G to stand for a glucose molecule, then starch or cellulose can be represented as:

-G-G-G-G-G-G-G-G-G-G-G-G-G- G-G-G-G-G-G-G-G-G-G-G-G-G-G-

Again, a real molecule of starch or cellulose contains hundreds or thousands of these G units.

Synthetic polymers

Scientists began to make synthetic polymers long before they really understood the structure of these giant molecules. As early as the 1860s, chemists were exploring ways in which naturally occurring polymers such as cellulose could be modified to make them more useful. These polymers eventually became known as plastics. The term comes from the fact that most early polymers could be melted, bent, and shaped.

The first truly synthetic polymer was invented around 1910 by Belgian-American chemist Leo H. Baekeland (1863–1949). Baekeland reacted phenol with formaldehyde to produce a tough, hard, material that did not dissolve in water or other solvents and that did not conduct an electric current. He named the product Bakelite. Bakelite rapidly became very popular as casing material for a number of household products, such as telephones and electrical appliances.

Credit for first recognizing the chemical nature of polymers is usually given to German chemist Hermann Staudinger (1881–1965). In 1926, Staudinger suggested that polymers are very large molecules consisting of one or two simple units (the monomers) repeated over and over again. He received the Nobel Prize in chemistry in 1953 for this discovery.

Products made of polyvinyl chloride, a synthetic polymer. *(Reproduced by permission of Photo Researchers, Inc.)*

In the last half of the twentieth century, chemists invented dozens of different kinds of synthetic polymers. Most of these compounds were developed to have certain special and desirable properties, such as toughness; resistance to wear; low density; resistance to water, acids, bases, and other chemicals; and resistance to the flow of electric current.

[*See also* **Plastics**]

Precious metals

The precious metals—gold, silver, and platinum—have historically been valued for their beauty and rarity. Ancient people considered gold and silver to be of noble birth compared to the more abundant metals. Chemists have retained the term noble to indicate the resistance these metals have to corrosion and their natural reluctance to combine with other elements.

The course of recorded human history shows twists and turns influenced to a large degree by precious metals. It was Greek silver that gave Athens its Golden Age, Spanish gold and silver that powered the Roman Empire's expansion, and the desire for gold that motivated Columbus to sail west across the Atlantic. The Spanish exploration of Latin America was also driven in large part by the search for gold. Small amounts of gold found in North Carolina, Georgia, and Alabama played a role in the 1838 decision to remove the Cherokee nation to Oklahoma. The California gold rush of 1849 made California a state the following year, and California gold fueled northern industry and backed up Union currency, two major factors in the outcome of the American Civil War (1861–65).

Gold

Since ancient times, gold has been associated with the Sun. Its name is believed to be derived from a Sanskrit word meaning "to shine," and its chemical symbol (Au) comes from *aurum,* Latin for "glowing dawn." Pure gold has an exceedingly attractive, deep yellow color. It is soft enough to scratch with a fingernail, and it is the most malleable of metals. A block of gold about the size of a sugar cube can be beaten into a translucent film some 27 feet (8 meters) on a side. Gold's purity is expressed either as fineness (parts per 1,000) or in karats (parts per 24). An alloy (mixture of two or more metals with properties different from those of the metals of which it is made) containing 50 percent gold is 500 fine or 12 karat. Gold resists corrosion by air and most chemicals, but it can

Words to Know

Alloy: A mixture of two or more metals with properties different from those of the metals of which it is made.

Catalyst: A compound that speeds up the rate of a chemical reaction without undergoing any change in its own composition.

Compound: A substance consisting of two or more chemical elements in specific proportions.

Hydrothermal fluid: Underground hot water-rich fluid capable of transporting metals in solution.

Malleable: Capable of being rolled or hammered into thin sheets.

Ore: Mineral compound that is mined for one of the elements it contains, usually a metal element.

Placer: A gravel or sand deposit left by a river containing a concentration of heavy mineral grains such as gold or platinum.

be dissolved in a mixture of nitric and hydrochloric acids, a solution called *aqua regia* because it dissolves the "king of metals."

Gold is so rare that one ton of average rock contains only about eight pennies worth of gold. Gold ore (an ore is a mineral compound that is mined for one of the elements it contains, usually a metal element) occurs where geologic processes have concentrated gold to at least 250 times the value found in average rock. At that concentration, there is still one million times more rock than gold and the gold is rarely seen. Ore with visible gold is incredibly valuable. Gold most commonly occurs as a pure metal called native gold or as a natural alloy with silver called electrum. Gold is found in a wide variety of geologic settings, but placer gold and gold veins are the most economically important.

Placer gold is derived from gold-bearing rock from which the metal has been freed by weathering. Gravity and running water then combine to separate the dense grains of gold from the much lighter rock fragments. Rich concentrations of gold can develop above deeply weathered gold veins as the lighter rock is washed away. Gold washed into mountain streams forms placer deposits where the stream slows enough to deposit the gold. Placer gold is also found in gravel bars where it is deposited along with much larger rocky fragments. The discovery of placer gold set off the California gold rush of 1849 and the rush to the Klondike in 1897. The largest river placers known are in Siberia, Russia. Gold-rich sands there are removed with jets of water, a process known as hydraulic mining.

Vein gold is deposited by hot subterranean water known as a hydrothermal fluid. Hydrothermal fluids circulate through rock to leach (dissolve out) small amounts of gold from large volumes of rock and then deposit it in fractures to form veins. Major United States gold vein deposits have been discovered at Lead in the Black Hills of South Dakota and at Cripple Creek on the slopes of Pikes Peak, Colorado. Important vein deposits are also found in Canada and Australia.

Gold's virtual indestructibility means that almost all the gold ever mined is still in use. It is entirely possible that some gold atoms that once graced the head of Egyptian queen Cleopatra (69–30B.C.) now reside in someone's jewelry, stereo, or teeth today. Gold is being mined in ever-increasing amounts from increasingly lower-grade deposits. It is estimated

One ton of gold bars. *(Reproduced by permission of Photo Researchers, Inc.)*

that 70 percent of all gold recovered has been mined since the beginning of the twentieth century. Each year, nearly 2,000 tons (1,800 metric tons) are added to the total. Nevada currently leads the United States in gold production, while the Republic of South Africa is the world's leading gold-producing nation.

Gold has traditionally been used for coins, bullion, jewelry, and other decorative items. Because of its chemical properties, gold is nonallergenic and remains tarnish-free indefinitely. For much the same reasons, gold has long been used in dentistry. Modern industry employs increasing quantities of gold, mostly for use as electrical contacts in microcircuits.

Silver

Silver is a brilliant white metal and the best metal in terms of thermal (heat) and electrical conductivity. Its chemical symbol, Ag, is derived from its Latin name, *argentum,* meaning "white and shining." Silver is not nearly as precious, dense, or noble as gold or platinum. The ease with which old silverware tarnishes is an example of its chemical reactivity. Although native silver is found in nature, it most commonly occurs in compounds with other elements, especially sulfur.

Hydrothermal veins constitute the most important source of silver. The Comstock Lode, located 15 miles (24 kilometers) southeast of Reno, Nevada, is a well-known example. Hydrothermal silver veins are formed in the same manner as gold veins, and the two metals commonly occur together. Silver, however, being more reactive than gold, can be leached from surface rocks and carried downward in solution. This process can concentrate silver into exceedingly rich deposits deep underground.

Mexico has traditionally been the world's leading silver producing country, but the United States, Canada, and Peru each contribute significant amounts. Vast quantities of silver are used in jewelry, silverware, and coins, but even larger amounts are used in products of the photographic and electronics industries.

Platinum

Platinum, like silver, is a beautiful silver-white metal. Its chemical symbol is Pt, and its name comes from the Spanish world for silver (*plata*), with which it was originally confused. Like gold, it can be found in pure metallic chunks in stream placers.

Platinum commonly occurs with five similar metals known as the platinum group metals. The group includes osmium, iridium, rhodium, palladium, and ruthenium. All are rare, expensive, and classified chemically as noble metals. Platinum is found as native metal, natural alloys, and as compounds with sulfur and arsenic. Platinum ore deposits are rare and highly scattered. Nearly half the world's historic production of platinum comes from the Republic of South Africa.

Platinum is used mostly in catalytic converters for pollution control on automobiles. Low-voltage electrical contacts form the second most common use for platinum, followed closely by dental and medical applications, including dental crowns and a variety of pins and plates used internally to secure human bones. Platinum is also used as a catalyst in the manufacture of explosives, fertilizer, gasoline, insecticides, paint, plastic, and pharmaceuticals.

[*See also* **Minerals; Mining**]

Pressure

Pressure is the amount of force applied to a given area. Pressure is expressed in units such as pounds per square inch in the English system or newtons per square meter in the metric system.

To understand the difference between force and pressure, consider a block of wood one foot on each side and weighing 40 pounds. The force exerted by that block of wood on a table top is equal to its weight: 40 pounds. But the pressure exerted by the wood is the force exerted on each square inch. Since the block of wood rests on an area of 144 square inches (12 inches by 12 inches), the pressure it exerts is 40 pounds ÷ 144 square inches = 0.28 pounds per square inch.

But now imagine that the same block of wood is cut apart and put back together in the shape of a pyramid. And imagine that a way can be found to balance that pyramid of wood on the table top on its point. Then, the pressure exerted by the wood block is quite different. Its weight remains the same, 40 pounds, but all of that weight rests on a single point. Imagine that the area of the point is 0.01 square inch. Then, the pressure exerted by the block is 40 pounds ÷ 0.01 square inch = 4,000 pounds per square inch.

Perhaps you can see why a sharp knife cuts better than a dull one, or why a nail has a sharp point rather than a flat one. The force exerted by the knife or the nail is focused on a small area, creating a large pressure and, therefore, a more effective cutting or driving force.

All forms of matter—solid, liquid, and gas—exert pressure. In the case of solids and liquids, that pressure is caused by the weight of an object and the area on which that weight acts. In the case of a gas, that pressure is caused by the motion of the gas particles. As gas particles travel through space, they collide with walls, table tops, ceilings, floors, and other objects. The collision of the gas particles against these objects causes gas pressure.

Atmospheric pressure

The form of pressure best known to most people is probably air pressure. Air exerts pressure, as do all gases, because of the movement of air particles and their collision with other objects. At sea level, this pressure has a value of approximately 760 millimeters of mercury (760 mm Hg). This unit may seem peculiar, but it represents the height of a column of mercury that can be held up by air pressure at sea level.

Atmospheric pressure is also measured in other units such as atmospheres, millibars, inches of mercury, and kilopascals. One atmosphere of pressure is equal to 760 mm Hg; 29.92 inches of mercury; 1013.25 millibars; or 101.3 kilopascals.

Atmospheric pressure depends on a number of factors, including altitude and weather conditions. In general, the higher one goes in the atmosphere, the lower the atmospheric pressure. Also, the greater the humidity (amount of moisture in the air), the lower the atmospheric pressure.

Primates

The mammals (warm-blooded animals) called primates include the lower primates (lemurs, lorises, and tarsiers) and the higher primates (monkeys, apes, and humans). Mostly occurring in tropical areas, primates first evolved more than 50 million years ago from shrewlike, insect-eating mammals. Many present-day primates are arboreal (tree-dwellers), with long, agile limbs for climbing and four fingers and an opposable thumb covered by nails for grasping branches. (An opposable thumb is one that is able to be placed against the other fingers.) The eyes of primates are located in the front of their heads, allowing depth perception. Their diet consists of fruit, leaves, stems, buds, and insects, although some primates are carnivores (meat-eaters). Primates have large brains, with the higher primates showing a marked intelligence.

Words to Know

Arboreal: Living in trees.

Diurnal: Occurring or active during the daytime.

Nocturnal: Occurring or active at night.

Opposable thumb: A thumb that occurs opposite the fingers so that it can be placed against them to grasp objects.

Lower primates: Lemurs, lorises, tarsiers

The lower primates, including the lemurs, lorises, and tarsiers, were the first primates, occurring in North America, Europe, and Asia. Lemurs now occur only on Madagascar, an island off the coast of Africa. They are mostly tree-dwelling, nocturnal (active at night) animals with a moist snout (nose) and a long, furry tail. Lorises are slow-moving, tailless, and nocturnal and live in trees. They are found in southeast Asia and Africa. Tarsiers are small primates with large bulging eyes and a long, thin, naked tail. They are mainly tree-dwelling, nocturnal creatures of the islands of southeast Asia.

Higher primates: Monkeys, apes, humans

Monkeys are mostly tree-dwelling, social mammals that are chiefly diurnal (active during daytime). Old World monkeys (those originating in Africa and Asia) have narrow nostrils that face downward, a fully opposable thumb, and average-sized or absent tails. Included in this group are the baboons and macaques, which are ground-dwellers. New World monkeys (those originating in Central and South America) have rounded nostrils set fairly far apart. Their thumbs are smaller than Old World monkeys, and they typically have long arms and legs and long tails for wrapping around tree limbs. Spider monkeys, marmosets, and capuchins are examples of New World monkeys.

Apes—the group of primates most closely related to humans—include gorillas, orangutans, chimpanzees, and gibbons. The hands, feet, and face of an ape are hairless, while the rest of its body is covered with coarse black, brown, or red hair.

Gorillas are ground-dwelling mammals that inhabit the forests of central Africa. They are the largest and most powerful of all primates, reaching a length of 6 feet (1.8 meters) and weighing up to 500 pounds (227 kilograms).

Orangutans are chestnut-colored, long-haired apes live only in the rain forests of the Indonesian islands of Sumatra and Borneo. They are the largest living arboreal mammals, spending the daylight hours moving through the forest canopy in search of fruit, leaves, tree bark, and insects. Many orangutans live to 50 or 60 years of age.

Chimpanzees are partly arboreal, partly ground-dwelling primates that live in the forests of west, central, and east Africa. They are agile creatures that can move rapidly through treetops. On the ground, chimpanzees usually walk on all fours (called knuckle-walking), since their arms are longer than their legs. They make and use a variety of tools, throw sticks and stones as weapons, and hunt and kill young monkeys. Chimpanzees are the most intelligent of the apes and are capable of learning complex sign language. Their closest relatives are humans, who share much of the same genetic material.

A Philippine tarsier. *(Reproduced by permission of Photo Researchers, Inc.)*

An orangutan in Borneo, Indonesia. *(Reproduced by permission of Photo Researchers, Inc.)*

Gibbons are the smallest of the apes and are found in southeast Asia, China, and India. They spend most of their lives at the tops of trees in the jungle, using their long arms to swing their agile bodies from tree to tree in search of leaves and fruit. Gibbons are known for their loud calls and songs, which they use to defend their territory. They are devoted parents who show extraordinary affection in caring for offspring.

Humans and their related ancestors belong to a group called hominids, primates with an upright posture and bipedal (two-footed) locomotion. Humans differ from apes in that their brains are larger in relation to their bodies and their faces are flatter and do not have a bony ridge over the eyes. The human skeleton is similar to that of a chimpanzee or gorilla but is modified for walking on two legs. Also, human teeth are smaller than those of apes, with the canine teeth much less pronounced.

Bridging the gap between lower and higher primates

The human line split off from the one leading to chimpanzees and apes 5 million to 7 million years ago. Scatterings of fossils have led scientists to speculate that the earliest primates of any kind appeared about 55 million years ago, mainly in Asia. But just when the two lines of primates (lower and higher) separated had seemed to be lost in the wide gaps in the fossil record.

In March 2000, however, scientists announced they had discovered the fossil bones of an animal they believed to be the earliest known relative in the primate lineage that led to monkeys, apes, and humans. The animal, which the scientists named Eosimias for "dawn monkey," lived some 45 million years ago in a humid rain forest in what is now China. The smallest primate ever found, alive or extinct, it was no bigger than the length of a human thumb and weighed less than 1 ounce (28 grams). It was also probably nocturnal and solitary and fed on insects and fruits. Scientists believe Eosimias to be a transitional figure when lower primates, known as prosimians, went their separate way, eventually developing into present-day lemurs, lorises, and tarsiers. Eosimias was part of the diverging higher primates, known as anthropoids, that eventually evolved into today's monkeys, apes, and humans.

Probability theory

Probability theory is a branch of mathematics concerned with determining the likelihood that a given event will occur. This likelihood is determined by dividing the number of selected events by the number of total events possible. For example, consider a single die (one of a pair of dice) with six faces. Each face contains a different number of dots: 1, 2, 3, 4, 5, or 6. If you role the die in a completely random way, the probability of getting any one of the six faces (1, 2, 3, 4, 5, or 6) is one out of six.

Probability theory originally grew out of problems encountered by seventeenth-century gamblers. It has since developed into one of the most respected and useful branches of mathematics with applications in many different industries. Perhaps what makes probability theory most valuable is that it can be used to determine the expected outcome in any situation—from the chances that a plane will crash to the probability that a person will win the lottery.

History of probability theory

Probability theory was originally inspired by gambling problems. The earliest work on the subject was performed by Italian mathematician and physicist Girolamo Cardano (1501–1576). In his manual *Liber de Ludo Aleae,* Cardano discusses many of the basic concepts of probability complete with a systematic analysis of gambling problems. Unfortunately, Cardano's work had little effect on the development of probability because his manual did not appear in print until 1663—and even then received little attention.

The probability of rolling snake eyes (two ones) with a pair of dice is 1 in 36. *(Reproduced by permission of Field Mark Publications.)*

In 1654, another gambler named Chevalier de Méré invented a system for gambling that he was convinced would make money. He decided to bet even money that he could roll at least one twelve in 24 rolls of two dice. However, when the Chevalier began losing money, he asked his mathematician friend Blaise Pascal (1623–1662) to analyze his gambling system. Pascal discovered that the Chevalier's system would lose about 51 percent of the time.

Pascal became so interested in probability that he began studying more problems in this field. He discussed them with another famous mathematician, Pierre de Fermat (1601–1665) and, together they laid the foundation of probability theory.

Methods of studying probability

Probability theory is concerned with determining the relationship between the number of times some specific given event occurs and the number of times any event occurs. For example, consider the flipping of a coin. One might ask how many times a head will appear when a coin is flipped 100 times.

Determining probabilities can be done in two ways: theoretically and empirically. The example of a coin toss helps illustrate the difference between these two approaches. Using a theoretical approach, we reason that in every flip there are two possibilities, a head or a tail. By assuming each event is equally likely, the probability that the coin will end up heads is $\frac{1}{2}$ or 0.5.

The empirical approach does not use assumptions of equal likelihood. Instead, an actual coin flipping experiment is performed, and the number of heads is counted. The probability is then equal to the number of heads actually found divided by the total number of flips.

Basic concepts

Probability is always represented as a fraction, for example, the number of times a "1 dot" turns up when a die is rolled (such as 1 out 6, or 1/6) or the number of times a head will turn up when a penny is flipped (such as 1 out of 2, or $\frac{1}{2}$). Thus the probability of any event always lies somewhere between 0 and 1. In this range, a probability of 0 means that there is no likelihood at all of the given event's occurring. A probability of 1 means that the given event is certain to occur.

Probabilities may or may not be dependent on each other. For example, we might ask what is the probability of picking a red card OR a king from a deck of cards. These events are independent because even if you pick a red card, you could still pick a king.

As an example of a dependent probability (also called a conditional probability), consider an experiment in which one is allowed to pick any ball at random out of an urn that contains six red balls and six black balls. On the first try, a person would have an equal probability of picking either a red or a black ball. The number of each color is the same. But the probability of picking either color is different on the second try, since only five balls of one color remain.

Applications of probability theory

Probability theory was originally developed to help gamblers determine the best bet to make in a given situation. Many gamblers still rely on probability theory—either consciously or unconsciously—to make gambling decisions.

Probability theory today has a much broader range of applications than just in gambling, however. For example, one of the great changes that took place in physics during the 1920s was the realization that many events in nature cannot be described with perfect certainty. The best one can do is to say how *likely* the occurrence of a particular event might be.

When the nuclear model of the atom was first proposed, for example, scientists felt confident that electrons traveled in very specific orbits around the nucleus of the atom. Eventually they found that there was no basis for this level of certainty. Instead, the best they could do was to specify the probability that a given electron would appear in various regions of space in the atom. If you have ever seen a picture of an atom in a science or chemistry book, you know that the cloudlike appearance of the atom is a way of showing the probability that electrons occur in various parts of the atom.

Proof

A proof is a logical argument demonstrating that a specific statement, proposition, or mathematical formula is true. It consists of a set of assumptions (also called premises) that are combined according to logical rules in order to establish a valid conclusion. This validation can take one of two forms. In a direct proof, a given conclusion can be shown to be true. In an indirect proof, a given conclusion can be shown not to be false and, therefore, presumably to be true.

Direct proofs

A direct proof begins with one or more axioms or facts. An axiom is a statement that is accepted as true without being proved. Axioms are also called postulates. Facts are statements that have been proved to be true to the general satisfaction of all mathematicians and scientists. In either case, a direct proof begins with a statement that everyone can agree with as being true. As an example, one might start a proof by saying that all healthy cows have four legs. It seems likely that all reasonable people would agree that this statement is true.

The next step in developing a proof is to develop a series of true statements based on the beginning axioms and/or facts. This series of statements is known as the argument of the proof. A key factor in any proof is to be certain that all of the statements in the argument are, in fact, true statements. If such is the case, one can use the initial axioms and/or facts and the statements in the argument to produce a final statement, a proof, that can also be regarded as true.

As a simple example, consider the statement: "The Sun rises every morning." That statement can be considered to be either an axiom or fact. It is unlikely that anyone will disagree it.

One might then look at a clock and make a second statement: "The clock says 6:00 A.M." If we can trust that the clock is in working order, then this statement can be regarded as a true statement—the first statement in the argument for this proof.

The next statement might be to say that "6:00 A.M. represents morning." Again, this statement would appear to be one with which everyone could agree.

The conclusion that can be drawn, then, is: "The Sun will rise today." The conclusion is based on axioms or facts and a series of two true statements, all of which can be trusted. The statement "The Sun will rise today" has been proved.

Indirect proofs

Situations exist in which a statement cannot be proved easily by direct methods. It may be easier to disprove the opposite of that statement. For example, suppose we begin with the statement "Cats do not meow." One could find various ways to show that that statement is not true—that it is, in fact, false. If we can prove that the statement "Cats do not meow" is false, then it follows that the opposite statement "Cats meow" is true, or at least *probably* true.

Prosthetics

Prosthetics (pronounced prahs-THEH-tiks) is the branch of medicine that deals with the artificial replacement of a missing body part. A prosthesis (pronounced prahs-THEE-sis) is the general term for the artificial part itself that replaces the body part usually lost to disease or injury. Prosthetics has a long history, and recent design advances that use battery power and new lightweight composite materials are making prostheses better and easier to use.

History

Although nothing can ever fully replace any part of our bodies, most people who have suffered the loss of a body part or who were born missing something that everyone else has and needs—like a foot or a hand—would agree that something is usually better than nothing. People have used all sorts of artificial devices probably from the beginnings of human history to help them compensate for the loss of a limb. Thus in very ancient times, the first and simplest prosthesis may have been a forked tree limb that was used as a crutch to help someone walk whose leg may have been badly damaged or lost in an accident or to a disease.

The known history of prosthetics or designing and making prostheses goes back at least to 300 B.C., from which time we have evidence of crude devices being made to replace a missing lower leg. These consisted of metal plates being hammered over a wooden core, which was then strapped to the stump of the remaining leg. These very early prostheses were usually made by blacksmiths, armor makers, and other artisans who were skilled at using metal, wood, and leather.

One of the earliest written references to prosthetics is found in a book published in France in 1579. That year, French surgeon Ambroise Paré (1510–1590) published his complete works, part of which described some of the artificial limbs he fitted on his amputees. As a military surgeon, Paré had removed many a soldier's shattered arm or leg, and he eventually began designing and building artificial limbs to help the men who had been maimed. Once Paré's work became better known, others tried to follow his lead. German history tells of the Knight of the Iron Hand who had lost his arm in battle, but who was fitted with an artificial arm that had gears and levers that moved his metal fingers. It is said that he became an even fiercer warrior with his new arm. By the 1700s, metal hooks attached by a wooden or leather shell and leather straps were being use to replace missing hands. In the next century, articulated joints or those that could bend began to replace the stiff solid limb.

Wartime advances

Wartime always pushes surgery beyond its limits, and it is not surprising that most of the advances in prosthetics have taken place during wars. The American Civil War (1861–65) was especially gruesome when it came to maiming healthy young men, and over 30,000 amputations were performed on the Union side alone. A manufacturer in New York priced its wooden socket limbs anywhere from $75 to $150. Most of these prostheses differed little from those of a century before, and it was not until the two twentieth-century world wars that any real progress was made in the design and manufacture of artificial limbs.

During and after World War II (1939–45), newer and lighter materials like plastics and aluminum were joined to newly updated mechanical joints, and for the first time, prostheses became more comfortable and easier to use. With postwar research supported by the U.S. Veteran's Administration, mechanical arms were developed whose hook end could open or close with a shrug of the shoulder. Advances were also made in above-knee and below-knee devices for amputees. Following the Vietnam War during the 1960s and 1970s, a new wave of needy amputees spurred further refinements in prosthetics, and by then electronic control was being introduced.

Many types of prostheses

It should be noted that the term prosthetics does not refer only to the replacement of lost arms or legs. In fact, the word prosthesis includes any artificial body part, and therefore includes everything from a set of false teeth to an artificial breast for women who have undergone a mastectomy (pronounced mass-TEK-tuh-mee) or breast removal. However, the fact that the amputee population in the United States alone ranges somewhere between 400,000 and 1,000,000 makes those in need of a limb predominate. This is especially so since nine out of ten of these amputations involve the leg from the foot to the knee. Further, three-fourths of these amputations are necessitated by disease, usually cancer or a circulation disease associated with diabetes. The remainder are caused by accidents, with a very small percentage being due to birth defects.

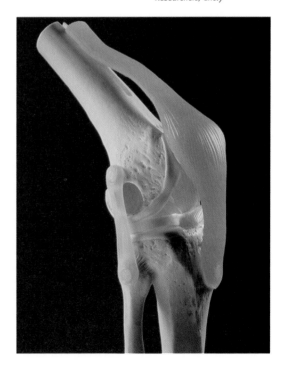

An artificial knee joint made out of plastic. *(Reproduced by permission of Photo Researchers, Inc.)*

Modern advances in design

Given these numbers, it is obvious that there is a real need for new and better prostheses. Fortunately, the beginnings of a major change in design is taking place as composite materials—such as those that combine plastics and carbon fiber—are used more and more. These new materials are much stronger, lighter, and more durable than traditional materials. Silicon-based compounds are used to make artificial arms that are not only softer and more comfortable to wear than the old rigid plastic ones, but are also more real-looking. Often a person can have a mold made of a remaining limb, and a new one is cast to look just like its twin. These new limbs are also adjustable so they can be changed if the person gains weight or increases his or her level of activity. Further, amputees may have shock absorbers in their new knees, which can be made more and more flexible as they become more accustomed to their new leg.

Computers not only assist in the design and manufacture of some of these newer devices, but are being used to revolutionize all manner of prostheses as well. Amazingly, artificial eyes are being researched that will replace a damaged retina and allow certain blind people to see at least basic shapes and movements. Cochlear (pronounced COCK-lee-ur) implants stimulate the auditory nerve with electricity and allow certain deaf people to hear. These do not make sounds louder like hearing aids. Instead, an electrode in the inner ear bypasses the damaged part of the ear and creates a nerve impulse that stimulates the hearing part of the brain.

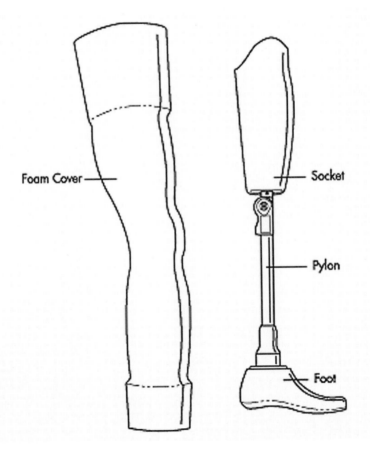

Foam Cover

Socket

Pylon

Foot

A typical above-the-knee prosthesis. *(Reproduced by permission of The Gale Group.)*

While some of these devices are astounding in the new or regained capabilities they provide, future systems presently being researched will be truly revolutionary. The goal of today's designers is to build an active device that works very much as our own muscles do. This means that for controlling movement, the ultimate goal is to tap into the nervous system itself and move naturally what are basically artificial muscles. Doing this is very difficult since it means being able to stimulate or detect signals from individual nerve cells. If this type of linkage is ever achieved, humans will be truly melded with a machine.

Besides the difficult problem of connecting with the brain's control system, the other great challenge is providing the power to run these bionic (pronounced by-ON-ik) implants. The energy requirements of any prosthesis are very important, and it appears that for decades to come, batteries of all types will still be used. However, continued battery improvements suggest that future prostheses will use electricity both to power and to control the artificial body part. Today, amputees are able to run races, peddle bicycles, and ski. In England, a man was fitted with the first fully powered electrical shoulder. Continued research and development in prosthetics suggests that life for an amputee will be closer to normal than ever before.

Protease inhibitors

Protease inhibitors (pronounced PRO-tee-ace in-HIH-bi-ters) are a new type of drugs that slow down the spread of HIV (human immunodeficiency virus) inside a person's body. HIV is the virus that causes the disease AIDS (acquired immunodeficiency syndrome). The drugs work by interrupting the way the AIDS virus uses a healthy cell to make copies of itself. Although not a cure for this disease, protease inhibitors have proven to be a powerful anti-HIV drug, especially when taken in combination with certain other drugs.

AIDS

AIDS is a contagious disease caused by a virus that disables the immune system, which is the body's natural defense against disease-causing organisms. HIV enters the body through the bloodstream, duplicates itself rapidly, and eventually destroys the body's immune system. This leaves the victim susceptible to other infectious diseases that usually prove fatal.

▼ Words to Know

AIDS (acquired immunodeficiency syndrome): A disease of the immune system believed to be caused by the human immunodeficiency virus (HIV). It is characterized by the destruction of a particular type of white blood cell and susceptibility to infection and other diseases.

Immune system: The body's natural defense system that guards against foreign invaders and that includes lymphocytes and antibodies.

Virus: A package of chemicals that are far smaller than the living cells they infect. Viruses are not classified as living organisms, since they cannot grow and reproduce on their own, but rely on a host cell to make copies of themselves.

AIDS cannot be spread by the type of casual contact that usually occurs between family and friends. HIV must somehow enter the bloodstream to infect a person, and the most common way for this to happen is through some form of sexual contact that allows bodily fluids from one person to enter that of another. This is what occurs during any type of sexual intercourse or sexual penetration of a person's body. Another way is for an infected intravenous drug user to share a needle with another person. HIV has also been transmitted to an unborn child by its infected mother, and until programs for blood screening were created, HIV had also been transmitted by blood transfusions.

How a virus works

Although there is no cure as yet for AIDS, scientists have discovered drugs that can slow down the spread of HIV once it gets into a person's body. They were able to do this by understanding how viruses work in the body. Like any other virus, HIV depends on the cell it first infects to make new copies of itself. Viruses cannot grow or reproduce on their own. Because of this, viruses are not even considered to be living organisms. However, when a virus infects a cell, it takes over the cell's metabolism, or the chemical reactions that go on inside, and basically gives a new set of instructions to the cell's command center. Once the cell obeys, and it must obey, the new virus copies then break out of the cell and go on to infect other cells, doing the same thing to them.

In people infected with HIV, there are over ten billion new copies of the virus made every day. So if the virus-copying is not stopped quickly, HIV spreads rapidly throughout the body. The AIDS virus has a favorite cell that it first attacks. This is known as the "T helper cell" or the "CD4 cell." These helper cells are important since they tell other infection-fighting cells to get working. Since HIV infects the helper cells first and destroys them, the body's natural immune system is eventually worn down and weakened. The victim eventually becomes susceptible to other infections that he or she would normally have no trouble resisting, and often, AIDS patients die from a variety of fungal, parasitic, or viral infections. It is when a person's helper cells drop below a certain level that an HIV infection becomes a case of AIDS.

How protease inhibitors work

Protease inhibitors are antiviral drugs that interrupt how HIV uses a healthy cell to make copies of itself. Studies of how HIV works have shown

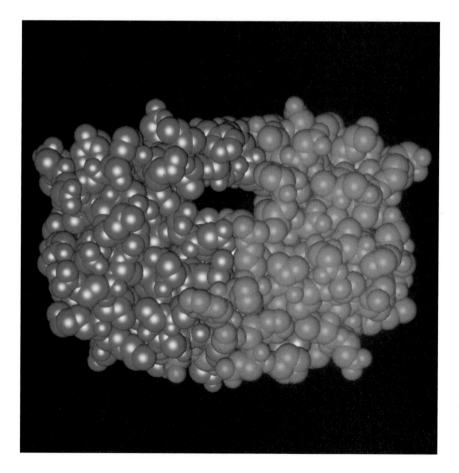

A computer graphic of the solids molecular model of a protease inhibitor. *(Reproduced by permission of Photo Researchers, Inc.)*

that the virus produces an enzyme or protein called protease that it must have to reproduce itself. Without protease, which cuts long chains of proteins and enzymes into shorter chains (which it needs to start the process), HIV cannot make copies of itself. The new class of drugs are called protease inhibitors because they "inhibit" or discourage something from happening. What they do specifically is to "gum up" the protease "scissors" so that they cannot do their cutting job. Protease inhibitors not only greatly reduce the number of new HIV copies that are made, they also make those that do manage to get produced defective in some way, so that they cannot go on and infect new cells. Although protease inhibitors are not a cure in that they cannot get rid of the HIV in an infected person' body, they can reduce the amount of virus in the blood by 99 percent.

Protease inhibitors were first developed by drug researchers in 1994, and a year later the U.S. Food and Drug Administration (FDA) approved the first version to be used in combination with other types of drugs that also worked at suppressing the spread of HIV in the cells. Since then, several types of protease inhibitors have been introduced and more are being studied. So far, protease inhibitors are the most powerful anti-HIV drugs available, allowing many people infected with the virus at least to try to live a somewhat normal life.

Although they do have some serious side effects and must be taken properly, the biggest problem with protease inhibitors may be the ability of HIV to learn how to resist them. Like any virus, HIV has the ability to change its chemical or genetic makeup and develop "resistance" to something that formerly used to defeat it. Researchers have found that once infected people stop their drug therapy, the virus rebounds in the body. So far, this means that people must continue the therapy throughout their lives. At present, researchers are not sure how long protease inhibitors will work in a person infected with HIV, but they are hopeful.

[*See also* **AIDS (acquired immunodeficiency syndrome)**]

Proteins

Proteins are very large molecules consisting of long chains of smaller units known as amino acids. Approximately two dozen different amino acids are used in the production of proteins. Suppose that we let the letter A stand for one amino acid, the letter B for a second amino acid, the letter C for a third amino acid, and so on through the two dozen amino acids. Then one simple way to represent a section of a protein is as follows:

Words to Know

Alpha helix: A type of secondary structure in which a chain of amino acids arranges itself in a three-dimensional spiral.

Photosynthesis: The process by which plants use light energy to manufacture their own food.

Primary structure: The linear sequence of amino acids making up a protein.

Quaternary structure: The highest level of structure found in proteins.

Secondary structure: Certain highly regular three-dimensional arrangements of amino acids within a protein.

Tertiary structure: A protein molecule's overall three-dimensional shape.

-A-B-N-E-Y-W-C-K-S-R-I-A-J-B-D-S-K-H-S-E-H-C-A-I-E-F-M-Q-I-A-S-

This representation actually shows only one small part of a protein molecule. Most proteins are very large molecules that contain hundreds or thousands of amino acids.

What proteins do

Proteins are extremely important components of all living organisms. The word protein itself means "primary importance" because of the many essential functions of proteins in cells. Much of our bodies' dry weight is protein. Even our bones are about one-quarter protein. The animals we eat and the microbes that attack us are likewise largely protein. The leather, wool, and silk clothing that we wear are nearly pure protein. The insulin that keeps diabetics alive and the "clot-busting" enzymes that may save heart attack patients are also proteins. Proteins can even be found working at industrial sites. Protein enzymes produce not only the high-fructose corn syrup that sweetens most soft drinks but also fuel-grade ethanol (alcohol) and other gasoline additives.

Within our bodies and those of other living organisms, proteins serve many functions. They digest foods and turn them into energy; they move molecules about within our cells; they let some substances pass through cell membranes while keeping others out; they turn light into chemical energy, making both vision and photosynthesis possible; they allow cells to detect and react to hormones and toxins in their surroundings; and they protect our bodies against foreign invaders.

Protein structure

The string of amino acids shown above represents only one level of protein structure, the simplest level. This structure is known as the protein's primary structure, and it is simply the linear sequence of amino acids in the protein.

All proteins have at least two more levels of structure. The amino acid groups that make up a protein all carry electrical charges. Those charges are responsible for the fact that some parts of the protein chain attract each other and other parts repel each other. The amino acid chain, therefore, always takes on some sort of three-dimensional structure. The most common of these structures is known as an alpha helix. Think of

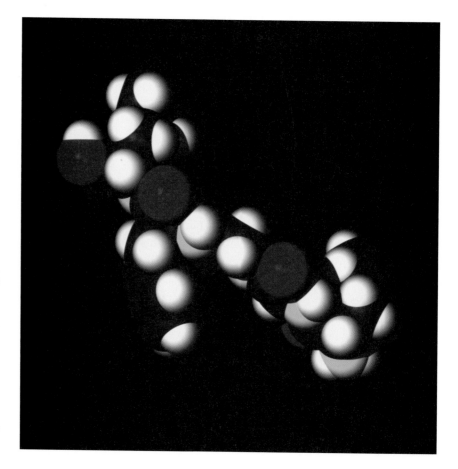

Computer graphic representation of a molecule of enkaphalin, a small protein molecule made up of five peptides, produced naturally in the human brain and by nerve endings elsewhere in the body. Enkephalin has a painkilling effect, and is thought to affect mood and stimulate motivation. *(Reproduced by permission of Photo Researchers, Inc.)*

what a Slinky™ toy or a spiral telephone cord looks like. Each of those structures is similar to an alpha helix. Many protein molecules have a similar three-dimensional spiral shape; this is known as the protein's secondary structure.

But proteins may take on even more complex structures. If you've ever played with a Slinky™, for example, you know that it can sometimes bend back on itself and twist into more complex shapes. The same can happen with protein molecules. The alpha helix secondary structure of the molecule can become bent and twisted into an even more complex shape, a shape known as the molecule's tertiary structure.

Some proteins have an even higher level of structure. One example is the protein known as hemoglobin. Hemoglobin makes up about a third of the weight of a red blood cell. It is responsible for transporting oxygen from the lungs to cells. Hemoglobin proteins have a quaternary structure in which four spiral amino acid chains are joined to each other through an iron atom in their midst.

Designer proteins

So-called "designer proteins" are synthetic (made in a lab) molecules invented by chemists to serve some specific function. At first, designer proteins were simply natural proteins in which modest changes were made by chemical reactions. These changes produced slight modifications in the physical, chemical, and biological properties of the protein.

For example, some proteins can be used as medicines, though they may also have undesirable side effects. By making small changes in the structure of the protein, chemists may be able to save the useful properties of the protein that make it valuable as a medicine while removing the undesirable side effects.

One long-term goal of many chemists is to design proteins from scratch. This process was still extremely difficult at the dawn of the twenty-first century and was expected to remain so until researchers better understood the way proteins form their tertiary structure. Nevertheless, scientists have been able to design a few small proteins whose stability or instability helps illuminate the rules by which proteins form. Building on these successes, researchers hope they may someday be able to design proteins for industrial and economic uses as well as for use in living organisms.

[*See also* **Amino acid; Antibody and antigen; Blood; Enzyme; Hormone; Metabolism; Nucleic acid**]

Protozoa

Protozoa are a varied group of single-celled animal-like organisms belonging to the kingdom Protista. More than 50,000 different types of protozoa have been described. Their name comes from two Greek words, *protos*, or "first," and *zoön*, or "animal." The vast majority of protozoa are microscopic, many measuring less than 1/200 millimeter. The largest, however, may reach 3 millimeters (0.1 inch) in length, large enough to be seen with the naked eye. Scientists have even discovered some fossil specimens that measured 20 millimeters (0.8 inch) in diameter.

Whatever their size, protozoa are well known for their diversity and the fact that they have evolved under so many different conditions. One of the basic requirements of all protozoa is the presence of water. Within this limitation, they may live in the sea; in rivers, lakes, or stagnant ponds of freshwater; in the soil; and even in decaying matter. Many are solitary organisms, but some live in groups. Some are free-living, while others are attached to other organisms. Some species are parasites of plants and animals, ranging from other protozoa to humans. Many protozoa form complex, exquisite shapes, although their beauty may be overlooked because of their very small size.

One protozoa splitting into two. *(Reproduced by permission of Photo Researchers, Inc.)*

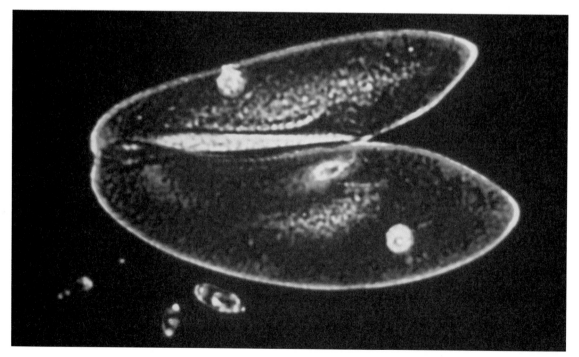

Words to Know

Chlorophyll: A green pigment that makes possible the conversion of carbon dioxide and water to complex carbohydrates.

Cilia: Tiny hairlike projections on the surface of a cell.

Cyst: A stage in a protozoan's life when it is covered by a tough outer shell and has become dormant.

Cytoplasm: The semifluid substance of a cell containing organelles and enclosed by the cell membrane.

Dormant phase: A period in which an organism is inactive.

Flagella: Whiplike structures used by some organisms for movement.

Heterotrophs: Organisms that cannot make their own food and that must, therefore, obtain their food from other organisms.

Parasitism: A situation in which one organism lives in connection with and at the expense of a second organism.

Protists: Members of the Kingdom Protista; primarily single-celled organisms that are not plants or animals.

Pseudopods: Extensions of an organisms cytoplasm used for movement and capturing food.

Symbiosis: A pattern in which two or more organism's live in close connection with each other, often to the benefit of both or all organisms.

Life patterns

The vast majority of protozoa are heterotrophic. That is, they cannot manufacture their own food, but must obtain it by eating other organisms. A few protozoa contain the green pigment chlorophyll, which allows them to make their own food.

All protozoa reproduce asexually, by dividing into two parts at regular intervals. Some species, however, have evolved the ability to reproduce sexually also.

Protozoa have evolved mechanisms that allow them to live under a great range of environmental conditions. When these conditions are unfavorable, most species are able to enter an inactive, or dormant, phase. They secrete a thick protective outer wall that prevents them from losing water and protects the cell from extreme temperatures. This tough little package, called a cyst, may also serve as a means of dispersal (to spread widely). Cysts are carried away on the wind or on the feet of animals. Once a cyst reaches a more favorable environment, its outer wall breaks down and the cell resumes normal activity.

Types of protozoa

Protozoa are classified according to the ways in which they move about. One phylum, the Sarcodina, moves by pushing out portions of their cytoplasm forming pseudopods, or "false feet." They capture their food by extending their pseudopods around it, engulfing it, and digesting it. Probably the best known example of the Sarcodina is the amoeba.

Members of the phylum Ciliophora get their name from tiny hair-like projections known as cilia on the surface of the cell. These protozoa swim around by waving their cilia back and forth, like the oars on a boat. Cilia are also used to obtain food. As they beat back and forth, the cilia create a whirlpoollike effect that brings food close enough for the organism to ingest. A common example of the ciliates is the paramecium.

The phylum Mastigophora consists of one-celled organisms that move about by means of flagella. Flagella are whiplike structures somewhat similar to cilia. The major difference between the two structures is that flagella are much larger than cilia. Also, flagellates have anywhere from one to several hundred flagella, while cilia never occur individually. The majority of flagellates live inside other organisms in either a symbiotic (mutually beneficial) or parasitic relationship. A well-known example of the flagellates is the organism that causes African sleeping sickness, the trypanosoma.

Members of the phylum Sporozoa have no means of movement. Instead, they form sporelike structures and attach themselves to other organisms. They are parasitic and depend on their hosts for all their food and survival. The best known of all Sporozoa are probably members of the genus *Plasmodium.* These organisms are responsible for malaria, a disease that is transmitted by the *Anopheles* mosquito.

[*See also* **Cell; Parasite; Plankton; Reproduction**]

Psychiatry

Psychiatry is the branch of medicine concerned with the study, diagnosis, and treatment of mental illnesses. The word psychiatry comes from two Greek words that mean "mind healing." Those who practice psychiatry are called psychiatrists. In addition to graduating from medical school, these physicians have postgraduate education in the diagnosis and treatment of mental behaviors that are considered abnormal.

Psychiatrists tend to view mental disorders as diseases and can prescribe medicine to treat those disorders. Other medical treatments occasionally used by psychiatrists include surgery (although rarely) and electroshock therapy.

Many, but not all, psychiatrists use psychoanalysis, a system of talking therapy based on the theories of Austrian psychiatrist Sigmund Freud (1856–1939). Freud believed that mental illness occurs when unpleasant childhood experiences are repressed (blocked out) because they are so painful. Psychoanalysts seek to cure patients by having them recover these repressed thoughts by talking freely until themes or issues related to the troubling conflicts arise, which are then addressed. Psychoanalysis often involves frequent sessions lasting over many years. Many psychiatrists use a number of types of psychotherapy in addition to psychoanalysis and prescription medication to create a treatment plan that fits a patient's needs.

History of psychiatry

The ancient Greeks believed people who were mentally ill had an imbalance of the elements (water, earth, air, and fire) and the humors (the bodily fluids of blood, phlegm, black bile, and yellow bile). In Europe during the Middle Ages (400–1450), most people thought that mental illness was caused by demonic possession and could be cured by exorcism. In the 1700s, French physician Philippe Pinel (1745–1826) became the first to encourage humane treatment for the mentally ill.

By the late 1800s, physicians started to take a more scientific approach to the study and treatment of mental illness. German psychiatrist Emil Kraepelin (1856–1926) had begun to make detailed written observations of how his patients' mental disturbances had come into being as well as their family histories. Freud began developing his method of using the psychoanalytic techniques of free association and dream interpretation to trace his patients' behavior to repressed, or hidden, drives. Others worked to classify types of abnormal behavior so that physicians could accurately diagnose patients.

Present-day psychiatry has become more specialized. Psychiatrists often focus on treating specific groups of people, such as children and adolescents, criminals, women, and the elderly.

Scientific researchers in the twentieth century have confirmed that many mental disorders have a biological cause. Those disorders can be treated effectively with psychiatric drugs that fall into four categories: antipsychotics (tranquilizers used to fight psychoses, or mental disorders characterized by loss of contact with reality), antidepressants, mood stabilizers, and antianxiety medications.

[*See also* **Depression; Multiple personality disorder; Phobias; Psychology; Psychosis; Schizophrenia**]

Psychology

Psychology is the scientific study of human and animal behavior, which includes both observable actions (such as eating and speaking) and mental activities (such as remembering and imagining). Psychology tries to understand why a person or animal behaves a certain way and then seeks to predict how that person or animal will behave in the future. For many years, psychology was a branch of philosophy (the study and exploration of basic truths governing the universe, nature, life, and morals [a sense of right and wrong]). In the nineteenth century, scientific findings established it as a separate field of scientific study.

A brief history

In 1879, German physiologist Wilhelm Wundt (1832–1920) established the first formal laboratory of psychology at the University of Leipzig in Germany. Wundt's work separated thought into simpler processes such as perception, sensation, emotion, and association. His approach looked at the structure of thought and came to be known as structuralism.

In 1890, American philosopher William James (1842–1910) published his *Principles of Psychology*. In contrast to structuralists, James thought consciousness (awareness) flowed continuously and could not be separated into simpler elements. James argued that studying the structure of the mind was not as important as understanding how it functions in helping us adapt to our surroundings. This approach became known as functionalism.

In the early 1900s, Austrian neurologist Sigmund Freud (1856–1939) began formulating psychoanalysis, which is both a theory of personality and a method of treating people with psychological difficulties. Freud's most influential contribution to psychology was his concept of the unconscious. He believed a person's behavior is largely determined by

▼ Words to Know

Behaviorism: School of psychology focusing on the environment and how it shapes behavior.

Cognitive psychology: School of psychology that focuses on how people perceive, store, and interpret information through such thought processes as memory, language, and problem solving.

Functionalism: School of psychology that focuses on the functions or adaptive purposes of behavior.

Gestalt psychology: School of psychology that focuses on perception and how the mind actively organizes sensations.

Humanistic psychology: School of psychology emphasizing individuals' uniqueness and their capacity for growth.

Neuropsychology: Study of the brain and nervous system and their role in behavior and mental processes.

Psychoanalysis: Theory of personality and method of psychotherapy founded by Sigmund Freud.

thoughts, wishes, and memories of which they are unaware. Painful childhood memories are pushed out of consciousness and become part of the *un*conscious. From here they can greatly influence behavior. As a method of treatment, psychoanalysis strives to bring these memories to awareness, freeing an individual from their often-negative influence.

In 1913, American psychologist John B. Watson (1878–1958) argued that mental processes could not be reliably located or measured. He believed that only observable, measurable behavior should be the focus of psychology. His approach, known as behaviorism, held that all behavior could be explained as a response to stimuli in the environment. Behaviorists tend to focus on the environment and how it shapes behavior.

At about the same time behaviorism arose, German psychologists Max Wertheimer (1880–1943), Kurt Koffka (1886–1941), and Wolfgang Köhler (1887–1967) founded Gestalt psychology (German for "form" or "configuration"). Gestalt psychologists argued that perception and thought cannot be broken into smaller pieces without losing their wholeness or essence. They argued that people actively organize information and that the wholeness and pattern of things dominates the way people perceive the world.

In the 1960s, American psychologists Abraham Maslow (1908–1970) and Carl Rogers (1902–1987) helped develop humanistic psychology. They felt that past psychological approaches had focused more on human weakness and mental illness. These previous approaches neglected mental strength and the potential for self-fulfillment. Maslow and Rogers believed that everyone has a basic need to achieve one's unique human potential.

Contemporary psychology

Much contemporary research has taken place in cognitive psychology. This school of psychology focuses on how people perceive, store, and interpret information, studying processes like memory, language, and problem solving. Unlike behaviorists, cognitive psychologists believe it is necessary to look at internal mental processes in order to understand behavior.

Advances in the knowledge of brain and nerve cell chemistry in the late twentieth century have influenced psychology tremendously. New technologies, which have produced visual images of the human brain at work, have allowed psychologists to study exactly where specific types of mental processes occur. This emerging field has been labeled neuropsychology or neuroscience.

[*See also* **Cognition; Psychiatry**]

Psychosis

A psychosis is a major psychiatric disorder characterized by the inability to tell what is real from what is not real. Hallucinations, delusions, and thought disorders can accompany psychosis. People who are psychotic often have a difficult time communicating with or relating to others. Sometimes they become agitated and violent. Among the conditions that include symptoms of psychosis are schizophrenia and manic depression (also known as bipolar disorder).

Psychotic episodes may last for a brief period or for weeks and months at a time. Psychosis can arise from emotional or organic causes. Organic causes include brain tumors, drug interactions, or drug or alcohol abuse. Since the 1950s, new medications have been developed to ef-

Words to Know

Delusions: Incorrect beliefs about reality that are clearly false.

Hallucinations: Seeing, feeling, hearing, or smelling something that does not exist in reality.

Manic depression: Also called bipolar disorder, a mental illness characterized by severe mood swings from depression to mania (great enthusiasm, energy, and joy).

Schizophrenia: A serious mental illness characterized by isolation from others and thought and emotional disturbances.

Synapses: Junctions between nerve cells in the brain where the exchange of electrical or chemical information takes place.

fectively treat psychosis, allowing a person suffering from delusions or hallucinations to regain a more accurate view of reality.

Forms of psychosis

Schizophrenia (skitz-o-FREN-ee-uh) is most frequently associated with psychosis. It is a mental illness that is characterized by delusions, hallucinations, thought disorders, disorganized speech and behavior, and sometimes catatonic behavior (an abnormal condition in which a person remains quiet and paralyzed). Emotions tend to flatten out (lose the normal peaks and valleys of happiness and sadness) and it becomes increasingly more difficult for the person to function normally in society.

Whereas schizophrenia is a thought disorder, manic-depressive disorder is a mood disorder. While the mood of a person suffering from schizophrenia is flat, the mood of a person suffering from manic depression can swing from great excitability to deep depression and feelings of hopelessness. Many manic-depressive patients also experience delusions and hallucinations.

Symptoms of psychosis

Hallucinations are a major symptom of psychosis and can be defined as sense perceptions that are not based in reality. Auditory hallucinations are the most common form. Patients hear voices that seem to be either outside or inside their heads. The voices may be argumentative or congratulatory. Patients who experience visual hallucinations may have an organic problem, such as a brain lesion. Other types of hallucinations involve the sense of smell and touch.

Delusions, incorrect beliefs about reality, are another symptom of psychosis. There are various types of delusions. Delusional patients may believe they are extremely important and powerful, or that they have a special relationship with a political leader, a Hollywood star, or God. Other delusional patients may feel they are being persecuted or mistreated by someone when no such persecution or mistreatment is taking place. Further delusions include unwarranted jealousy or the strongly held belief that one suffers from a disease or physical defect.

Medications for treatment

Antipsychotic drugs are prescription medications used to treat psychosis. The vast majority of antipsychotics work by blocking the absorption of dopamine, a chemical that occurs naturally in the brain. Dopamine is responsible for transmitting messages across the synapses, or junctions between nerve cells in the brain. Too much dopamine in a person's brain speeds up nerve impulses to the point of causing hallucinations, delusions, and thought disorders.

Antipsychotic medications were not used in the United States before 1956. Once these drugs, such as Thorazine™, were introduced, they gained widespread acceptance for the treatment of schizophrenia. The use of these drugs allowed the release of many people who had been confined to mental institutions.

Despite their benefits, antipsychotic medicines have a number of strong side effects. Among the most severe are muscle rigidity, muscle spasms, twitching, and constant movement. Perhaps the most serious side effect is neuroleptic malignant syndrome (NMS). This condition occurs when a patient taking an antipsychotic drug is ill or takes a combination of drugs. People suffering from NMS cannot move or talk. They also have unstable blood pressure and heart rates. Often, NMS is fatal.

Recently, a new generation of antipsychotic drugs has been developed as a result of discoveries about how the brain works. These new drugs have fewer side effects. Some do not completely block dopamine receptors; others are selective, blocking only one type of dopamine receptor.

[*See also* **Depression; Schizophrenia; Tranquilizer**]

Puberty

In humans, puberty is the period of physical development when sexual reproduction can first take place. It is characterized by maturity of the sexual organs and the development of secondary sexual characteristics (such as the deepening of a boy's voice or the development of a girl's breasts). The beginning of menstruation in females also begins in puberty. (Menstruation is the monthly cycle of the shedding of the lining of the uterus in women who are not pregnant.) The growth spurt experienced in puberty is characteristic of primates. Although other mammals may have increased reproductive organ growth, their overall size does not increase as dramatically.

Puberty marks the physical transition from childhood to adulthood. It usually occurs between the ages of 10 and 16, with females entering the stage earlier than males. Both sexes experience considerable increases in body height and weight during this period and require a balanced, nutritious diet with sufficient calories for optimal growth. Puberty usually lasts from two to five years and may be accompanied by emotional ups and downs.

Sexual development during puberty is regulated by the release of hormones (chemicals produced by the body that affect various bodily processes). The major control center that regulates the release of hormones in humans is the hypothalamus (a gland in the brain). The release of the hormone testosterone during puberty is associated with more aggressive behavior in males. Increases in estrogen (in females) and testosterone is associated with an increased sex drive, or libido.

Male puberty

During male puberty, the hypothalamus secretes hormones that stimulate the pituitary gland to release gonadotrophic hormones, which consist of follicle-stimulating hormone (FSH) and luteinizing hormone (LH). FSH stimulates development of the tubes in the testes in which sperm production takes place and is thought to be involved in sperm maturation. LH stimulates the testes to release testosterone. In males, puberty is marked by enlargement of the testicles and penis, lengthening of the vocal cords, which causes the voice to deepen, and growth of pubic hair. Facial hair may also begin to appear on the face, chest, and abdomen.

Female puberty

In females, puberty begins with the development of breasts and widening of the hips. Breast development can begin as early as 8 years

▼ Words to Know

Estrogens: Female sex hormones produced by the ovaries and involved in the development of reproductive organs and secondary sexual characteristics.

Fertility: The ability to produce offspring.

Hormone: A chemical produced in one part of the body that stimulates cellular activity in other body parts.

Hypothalamus: A part of the brain that regulates the production of hormones by the pituitary gland.

Menstruation: The cyclic shedding of the lining of the uterus in fertile women who do not become pregnant.

Ovary: One of a pair of female reproductive organs that produces eggs and sex hormones.

Pituitary gland: A gland located beneath the hypothalamus in the brain that secretes hormones controlling various bodily processes.

Primates: Mammals including monkeys, apes, and humans that have highly developed brains and hands with thumbs that are adapted for grasping.

Sperm: A male reproductive cell; semen.

Testes: The male reproductive organs that produce sperm and testosterone.

Testosterone: A male sex hormone that stimulates sperm production and is responsible for male sex characteristics.

of age but usually starts between 10 and 14. Full breast development may take two to five years. Pubic hair begins to grow shortly afterwards, followed by the first menstrual period, usually occurring between the ages of 10 and 14. Like male puberty, female puberty is initiated by hypothalamic hormones that stimulate the release of FSH and LH from the pituitary. FSH stimulates the development of follicles (sacs of cells in the ovaries in which eggs mature) and the secretion of reproductive hormones known as estrogens by the ovaries. Estrogens are involved in the growth of the uterus, development of the breasts, widening of the hips, and the distribution of fat and muscle. LH stimulates ovulation (the release of an egg from an ovary).

Sex and fertility

Puberty is a time when males and females begin to think about their sexuality and sexual activity. With sexual maturation comes fertility, meaning that females are now able to become pregnant and males' sperm are able to impregnate a female. Although teenagers' bodies may be sexually mature, the emotional maturity needed to engage in sexual activity and childrearing usually takes longer to develop.

[*See also* **Endocrine system; Hormone; Reproductive system**]

Pythagorean theorem

The Pythagorean theorem is one of the most famous theorems of geometry. It is often attributed to Pythagoras of Samos (Greece), who lived in the sixth century B.C. The theorem states that in any right triangle, the square of the hypotenuse of the triangle (the side opposite the right angle) is equal to the sum of the squares of the other two sides, or $c^2 = a^2 + b^2$.

This theorem was probably known long before the time of Pythagoras; it is thought to have been used by the ancient Egyptians and Babylonians. Nevertheless, Pythagoras (or some member of his school) is credited with the first proof of the theorem.

The converse of the Pythagorean theorem is also true. That is, if a triangle with sides a, b, and c has $c^2 = a^2 + b^2$, we know that the triangle is a right triangle.

Q

Qualitative analysis

Qualitative analysis is the process by which a chemist determines what chemical elements are present in a given sample of material. For instance, many people are now concerned about the presence of lead in our environment. Lead is a highly toxic element that can cause both mental and physical problems and, in high doses, even death. Suppose that a parent wants to know if the paint used on his or her house contains lead. That parent can take a sample of the paint to a chemist for qualitative analysis. That analysis will tell whether or not lead is present in the paint.

The science of qualitative analysis is based on the fact that every element and compound has distinctive properties such as melting point, boiling point, color, texture, density, and so on. Every element also reacts with other chemicals in very distinctive ways. For example, the lead used in house paints reacts with a compound known as hydrogen sulfide to form a distinctive black precipitate.

Identification of elements

In many instances, the question facing a chemist is similar to the lead problem described above: what element or elements are present in some unknown mixture. Chemists have developed a systematic method for answering that question. The method divides the most common chemical elements into about six groups. The elements are grouped in each case according to the way they react with some specific chemical. The three elements in Group I of the system, for example, are silver, lead, and mercury. These elements are grouped together because, when treated with hydrochloric acid, they all form a solid and precipitate out of solution.

The seven elements in Group II are grouped together because they all form precipitates with hydrogen sulfide. And so on.

Qualitative analysis is a process-of-elimination procedure. A chemist tests first for one group of elements (Group I) and makes a note of any elements found in this group. He or she then tests for a second group of elements (Group II) and makes a note of any additional elements found in this group. Eventually, every element is either identified or eliminated from consideration.

Instrumental methods

A number of mechanical devices have been invented to identify elements and compounds on the basis of certain physical properties. The mass spectrometer is one such instrument. In a mass spectrometer, an unknown material is first vaporized (converted into a gas) and then accelerated into the middle of a large magnet. The material travels along a curved path within the magnet and emerges onto a photographic plate. The shape of the path taken by the particles that make up the material and the point of impact they make on the photographic plate are determined by the mass and the velocity of the particles. (The term velocity refers both to the speed with which an object is moving and to the direction in which it is moving.) For example, helium atoms, hydrogen molecules, and chlorine molecules all travel through the magnet in distinctive pathways that can be recorded on the photographic plate. Chemists can study the photographic images made in a mass spectrograph and identify the particles that made those images.

Chromatography is another system for identifying the components of a mixture. In a chromatography column, a mixture of substances is allowed to pass through a long column containing some sticky material. Each component of the mixture has a different tendency to stick to the material. Chemists can look at the pattern of materials attached to the chromatography column and determine which substances were present in the original mixture.

One area in which qualitative analysis has become very important is the matching of human DNA tissue by law enforcement agencies to prove the presence or absence of a person at a crime scene.

[*See also* **Mass spectrometry; Radiation; Spectroscopy**]

Quantitative analysis

The term quantitative analysis is used to described any procedure by which the percentage composition of any compound or mixture is determined.

Words to Know

Classical (or wet) analysis: Those procedures in which a suitable chemical reagent is reacted with some unknown, either by precipitate formation or titration.

Gravimetric analysis: A classical quantitative technique in which a chemical added to an unknown forms an insoluble precipitate with some part of the unknown. The precipitate is then collected and weighed.

Instrumental analysis: Any quantitative technique in which some property of the unknown material (electrical, optical, thermal, etc.) is measured and related to the amount of the unknown present.

Volumetric analysis: A classical quantitative technique in which a solution of known concentration is reacted exactly with an unknown and a calculation is performed to find the amount of the unknown present.

For example, chemists might want to know the exact composition of some new compound that has been discovered. Or they might want to find out what the percentage of gold is in a new ore that has been discovered. Both of these questions can be answered by the procedures of quantitative analysis. Quantitative techniques can be divided into two general categories: wet or classical techniques and instrumental methods.

Classical methods

Classical methods have been used since the beginning of modern chemistry in the nineteenth century. They generally make use of balances and calibrated glass containers to measure the percentage composition of a compound or mixture. For example, the procedure known as gravimetric analysis involves the addition of some chemical to the unknown compound or mixture to produce a precipitate. A precipitate is a solid formed during a chemical reaction—usually in water—that eventually settles out of the solution. In a gravimetric analysis, the precipitate is filtered, washed, dried, and weighed. The composition of the original unknown can then be calculated from the weights of the precipitate and sample and original unknown.

Another classical form of quantitative analysis is known as volumetric analysis. Volumetric analysis uses a procedure known as titration, in which a solution whose concentration is known precisely is caused to react with an unknown sample. The amount of the known solution needed to react precisely with the sample of the unknown can be used to calculate the percentage composition of the unknown.

Instrumental methods

Suppose that you shine a beam of X rays at a sample of gold metal. Those X rays will cause electrons in gold atoms to become excited and give off light. The same result can be produced with any one of the 100 or so chemical elements. The only difference is that the electrons of each

Electron spectrometer being used for chemical analysis. (Reproduced by permission of Photo Researchers, Inc.)

element respond differently to the beam of X rays. This means that a chemist can decide which element or elements are present in a substance by shining X rays on the substance and observing the light pattern that is produced.

Forms of energy other than X rays can be used to produce the same results. For example, different elements conduct an electric current more or less effectively. In some cases, the presence of various elements in an unknown sample can be discovered, then, simply by passing an electric current through the sample and measuring the electrical conductivity in the sample.

Instrumental techniques have made possible a much greater sensitivity in the analysis of unknown materials. In most classical forms of analysis, an accuracy of about one part per thousand is not unusual (meaning one milligram of some substance is detectable in a one-gram sample).

Instrumental techniques have the capability to detect concentrations of one part per million, one part per billion, and, in the very best cases, one part per trillion. At that level of sensitivity, it would be possible to detect a grain of sand in an volume of water equal to about three typical high school swimming pools.

[*See also* **Spectroscopy**]

Quantum mechanics

Quantum mechanics is a method of studying the natural world based on the concept that waves of energy also have certain properties normally associated with matter, and that matter sometimes has properties that we usually associate with energy. For example, physicists normally talk about light as if it were some form of wave traveling through space. Many properties of light—such as reflection and refraction—can be understood if we think of light as waves bouncing off an object or passing through the object.

But some optical (light) phenomena cannot be explained by thinking of light as if it traveled in waves. One can only understand these phenomena by imagining tiny discrete particles of light somewhat similar to atoms. These tiny particles of light are known as photons. Photons are often described as quanta (the plural of quantum) of light. The term quantum comes from the Latin word for "how much." A quantum, or photon, of light, then, tells how much light energy there is in a "package" or "atom" of light.

Words to Know

Classical mechanics: A collection of theories and laws that was developed early in the history of physics and that can be used to describe the motion of most macroscopic objects.

Macroscopic: A term describing objects and events that can be observed with the five human senses, aided or unaided.

Photon: A unit of energy.

Quantum: A discrete amount of any form of energy.

Wave: A disturbance in a medium that carries energy from one place to another.

The fact that waves sometimes act like matter and waves sometimes acts like waves is now known as the principle of duality. The term duality means that many phenomena have two different faces, depending on the circumstances in which they are being studied.

Macroscopic and submicroscopic properties

Until the 1920s, physicists thought they understood the macroscopic properties of nature rather well. The term macroscopic refers to properties that can be observed with the five human senses, aided or unaided. For example, the path followed by a bullet as it travels through the air can be described very accurately using only the laws of classical physics, the kind of physics originally developed by Italian scientist Galileo Galilei (1564–1642) and English physicist Isaac Newton (1642–1727).

But the methods of classical physics do not work nearly as well—and sometimes they don't work at all—when problems at the submicroscopic level are studied. The submicroscopic level involves objects and events that are too small to be seen even with the very best microscopes. The movement of an electron in an atom is an example of a submicroscopic phenomenon.

In the first two decades of the twentieth century, physicists found that the old, familiar tools of classical physics produced peculiar answers or no answers at all in dealing with submicroscopic phenomena. As a result, they developed an entirely new way of thinking about and dealing with problems on the atomic level.

Uncertainty principle

Some of the concepts involved in quantum mechanics are very surprising, and they often run counter to our common sense. One of these is another revolutionary concept in physics—the uncertainty principle. In 1927, German physicist Werner Heisenberg (1901–1976) made a remarkable discovery about the path taken by an electron in an atom. In the macroscopic world, we always see objects by shining light on them. Why not shine light on the electron so that its movement could be seen?

But the submicroscopic world presents new problems, Heisenberg said. The electron is so small that the simple act of shining light on it will knock it out of its normal path. What a scientist would see, then, is not the electron as it really exists in an atom but as it exists when moved by a light shining on it. In general, Heisenberg went on, the very act of measuring very small objects changes the objects. What we see is not what they are but what they have become as a result of looking at them. Heisenberg called his theory the uncertainty principle. The term means that one can never be sure as to the state of affairs for any object or event at the submicroscopic level.

A new physics

Both the principle of duality and the uncertainty principle shook the foundations of physics. Concepts such as Newton's laws of motion still held true for events at the macroscopic level, but they were essentially worthless in dealing with submicroscopic phenomena. As a result, physicists essentially had to start over in thinking about the ways they studied nature. Many new techniques and methods were developed to deal with the problems of the submicroscopic world. Those techniques and methods are what we think of today as quantum physics or quantum mechanics.

[*See also* **Light; Subatomic particles**]

Quasar

Quasars are compact objects located far outside of our galaxy. They are so bright they shine more intensely than 100 galaxies combined, but they are so distant their light takes several billion years to reach Earth. Since the 1960s, astronomers have begun to come closer to the truth about these unusual phenomena in space.

The word quasar is a combined form of quasi-stellar radio sources. These objects are so named because they have been observed through

Words to Know

Big bang theory: Theory that explains the beginning of the universe as a tremendous explosion from a single point that occurred 12 to 15 billion years ago.

Black hole: Remains of a massive star that has burned out its nuclear fuel and collapsed under tremendous gravitational force into a single point of infinite mass and gravity.

Gamma rays: Short-wavelength, high-energy radiation formed either by the decay of radioactive elements or by nuclear reactions.

Infrared radiation: Electromagnetic radiation of a wavelength shorter than radio waves but longer than visible light that takes the form of heat.

Light-year: The distance light travels in one year, roughly 5.88 trillion miles (9.46 trillion kilometers).

Radiation: Energy transmitted in the form of electromagnetic waves or subatomic particles.

Radio telescope: A telescope that uses radio waves to create images of celestial objects.

Radio waves: Longest form of electromagnetic radiation, measuring up to six miles from peak to peak.

Redshift: Shift of an object's light spectrum toward the red end of the visible light range—an indication that the object is moving away from the observer.

Spectrum: Range of individual wavelengths of radiation produced when light is broken down by the process of spectroscopy.

Ultraviolet radiation: Electromagnetic radiation of a wavelength just shorter than the violet (shortest wavelength) end of the visible light spectrum.

radio telescopes. However, only about 10 percent of all quasars emit radio waves. The energy coming from quasars also includes visible light, infrared and ultraviolet radiation, X rays, and possibly even gamma rays.

In the early 1960s, American astronomer Allan Sandage photographed an area of the sky and noticed that one star had a very unusual spectrum. (A spectrum is the diagram of individual wavelengths of radiation from a star.) Most stars emit radiation consistent with the spectrum of ionized (electrically charged) hydrogen, the most abundant element on the surface of stars. This star, however, had a spectrum that seemed to reveal none of the elements known to exist in stars. The wavelengths at which it emitted radiation were heavily skewed toward the red-end range of visible light.

Such a skewed spectrum is known as redshift and is an indication of an object moving away from the point of observation. The greater the redshift, the faster the object is moving away. And as an object moves farther away, it picks up speed, increasing its redshift.

In 1963, Dutch astronomer Maarten Schmidt correctly identified the star's strange spectrum as that of a normal star with a high redshift. His calculations placed it an amazing two billion light-years away. In order to be observable from Earth at that distance, the object could not be a star, but had to be something larger, like a galaxy.

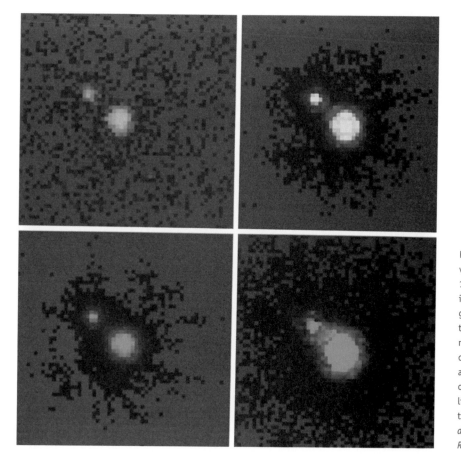

Hubble Space Telescope views of the distant quasar 120+101 indicate that its image has been split by gravitational lensing. Gravitational lensing is a phenomenon by which the pull of a massive object, such as a galaxy, can bend the light of another object when the light passes near or through the massive object. *(Reproduced by permission of Photo Researchers, Inc.)*

Schmidt measured the diameter of the object and learned that although it was emitting as much energy as one trillion suns, it was only about the size of the solar system. The brightest quasar to date, located in the constellation Draco, shines with the light of 1.5 quadrillion suns.

Origin of quasars

Astronomers formally believed that a quasar is found in a particular type of galaxy and is formed during the collision between two distant galaxies. When this happens, one galaxy creates a black hole in the other with the mass of about 100 million suns. (A black hole is a single point of infinite mass and gravity.) Gas, dust, and stars are continually pulled into the black hole. The temperature in the black hole then rises to hundreds of millions of degrees, and the black hole spews out tremendous quantities of radiation.

This theory was turned upside down in late 1996 when the Hubble Space Telescope (HST) took pictures of galaxies that are hosts to quasars. The pictures revealed that there was no pattern to the shapes and sizes of the galaxies. The pictures also showed that while many of the galaxies were colliding with each other as scientists had theorized, almost as many galaxies showed no signs of collision.

Quasars are the most distant, fastest, and most luminous large objects known in the universe. Because they are so far away, they give us a glimpse of the early universe. Since a light-year is a measure of the distance light travels in space in one year, viewing an object one billion light-years away is really like looking one billion years back in time. Some quasars are so distant they are virtually at the edge of time. They are relics from the period following the big bang event that created the universe some 12 to 15 billion years ago.

The most distant quasar known was discovered in November 1999 by the National Aeronautics and Space Administration's BATSE (Burst And Transient Source Experiment) satellite. Known by the scientific name 4C 71.07, this quasar appears to be about 11 billion light-years away. We therefore see quasar 4C 70.71 as it existed perhaps as little as a billion years after the big bang. That time period seems long by human standards, but it is near infancy by standards of the universe.

[*See also* **Big bang theory; Black hole; Galaxy; Redshift**]

R

Radar

Radar (a contraction of *ra*dio *d*etection *and* *r*anging) is an electronic system that measures the position, speed, or other characteristics of a far-off object by means of radio waves bounced off the surface of that object. It can pierce any atmospheric disturbance, such as a storm, all the way to the horizon. Within its range, radar can reveal clouds, a landmass, or objects such as ships, airplanes, or spacecraft. Radar can measure distance to a target object; for instance, aircraft use it to determine altitude. Radar is also used to monitor atmospheric systems, to track storms, and to help predict the weather. Military applications include weapons ranging (determining the distance from a weapon to a target) and direction in the control of guided missiles.

Basic radar operation

Light waves, radio waves, microwaves, and radar waves are all examples of electromagnetic waves. Unlike water waves, electromagnetic waves do not require a medium such as water or air to travel through. They can travel through a complete vacuum. Similar to light waves, radar waves bounce off some objects and travel through others.

The simplest mode of radar operation is range-finding, or determining how far away an object is. The radar unit sends radar waves out toward the target (radar systems can send out thousands of pulses per second). The waves hit the target and are reflected back. The returning wave is received by the radar unit, and the travel time is registered. According to basic principles of physics, distance is equal to the rate of travel (speed) multiplied by the time of travel. All electromagnetic waves travel at the same speed in a vacuum—the speed of light, which is 186,282 miles (299,727 kilometers) per second. This speed is reduced by a small amount when the waves are traveling through air, but this can be calculated.

Bats and dolphins are able to emit high-frequency sounds and orient (position) themselves by means of reflected sound waves. This ability is known as echolocation.

Radar and World War II

When the 1930s saw the possibility of a German air invasion, the English government accelerated its research into radar. A chain of radar stations was constructed that would throw an invisible net of radio waves over England. These waves could detect the approach and precise location of any aircraft.

When German dictator Adolf Hitler ordered a massive air strike against England in 1940, the radar shield worked. Although the German air force greatly outnumbered the British Royal Air Force, it was soundly beaten because the radar's eye could easily locate German planes, even in darkness and poor weather.

The military use of radar continued throughout World War II (1939–45). Compact transmitters were developed that could be mounted

A computer-generated three-dimensional perspective view of Death Valley, California, constructed from radar data from the Shuttle Imaging Radar-C (SIR-C) combined with an elevation map. The brightness levels seen here are determined by the radar reflecting on the surface. SIR-C was carried by a space shuttle in April 1994. *(Reproduced by permission of Photo Researchers, Inc.)*

on the underside of a plane to scan the ground far below for targets. Bombs and shells equipped with radar tracking systems were designed to "look" for their targets, exploding at just the right moment.

Other uses of radar

Radar devices began to trickle into everyday use soon after the end of the war. In 1947, a young engineer named John Barker attempted to use radar to regulate traffic lights. He noticed that a passing automobile would reflect a radio pulse, and that the speed of the vehicle could then be determined by examining the returning signal. Much to the dismay of speeders, Barker had devised the first radar speed-gun, now used by police worldwide.

Marine navigators, surveyors, meteorologists, and astronomers have also found uses for radar technology. A continuous-wave version called Doppler radar is often used to track storms and hurricanes. Probes launched into space have used radar to map the surfaces of other planets.

Radial keratotomy

Radial keratotomy is a type of eye surgery that is used to correct permanently myopia (pronounced my-O-pee-ah) or nearsightedness. In this surgery, a physician typically cuts slits into the cornea (pronounced KOR-nee-ah) with a tiny diamond scalpel, changing the shape of the cornea. The diamond scalpel is rapidly being replaced by laser surgery, which is quicker, more reliable, and has fewer complications.

How the eye works

The human eye can be considered a kind of extension of the brain. As an image-gathering tool, it can also be thought of as a camera, with the brain doing the developing of the picture. In many ways, a camera is similar to an eye in that both have a lens that can be focused for different distances. The retina (pronounced REH-tih-nuh), the innermost layer of the eye, can also be thought of as the film in the camera.

If looked at sideways, the human eyeball is spherical or round and has a bulge in the middle of its front. This outermost bulge or bump in its center is called the cornea. Described as a transparent (meaning light passes through) guard of the eye, the cornea is the first thing that receives the light that bounces off an image and goes into our eye. This is how human

Words to Know

Aqueous humor: Clear liquid filling the small cavities between the cornea and the iris and between the iris and the lens of the eye.

Cornea: The outer, transparent part of the eye through which light passes to the retina.

Nearsightedness: Vision disorder caused by an eyeball that is too long or a lens that is too strong; objects up close are seen easily while those far away appear blurry.

Retina: The light-sensitive part of the eyeball that receives images and transmits visual impulses through the optic nerve to the brain.

vision actually works, as our eyes detect light that is reflected from an object. The cornea is like a transparent front window that does the initial focusing for the eye. Although it is not nourished by blood, it is kept moist by a fluid called aqueous humor (pronounced AY-kwee-us HEW-mohr).

Shape of the cornea

The shape of the cornea is very important since it slows the light entering the eye and bends it toward the center of the eye where it meets the lens. Most of the focusing is done by the cornea, with the lens doing some fine tuning of the image. In general, the more curved the cornea is, the more it focuses. Myopia or nearsightedness (meaning that a person can see things better that are near than those that are far) is caused by eyeballs that are too "long" or too steeply curved. When this happens, the light rays are focused before they ever reach the retina, so that the image is out of focus or blurred by the time it does reach it.

Discovery of surgical procedure

The eye surgery called radial keratotomy is a procedure that changes the shape of the cornea (and therefore how it bends light) in order to correct its focusing errors. The surgery achieves this through microscopic radial cuts made in the cornea. The word "radial" describes the pattern of slits that "radiate" out from the center of the cornea like the spokes of a wheel. The word "keratotomy" is a compound Latin word in which "kera" means cornea and the suffix "totomy" means to cut. As long ago as 1869, a Dutch ophthalmologist (pronounced aaf-thaal-MA-low-jist) or eye doctor suggested that if the cornea could somehow be flattened by surgery, it might improve certain people's vision. He conducted a series of experiments on rabbits some years later. Although others in Norway, America, Italy, and Holland performed similar experiments around the beginning of the twentieth century, it was in Japan in the 1930s that a physician named Tsutomo Sato performed about 200 operations on people with mixed results.

Modern radial keratotomy was pioneered by Russian ophthalmologist Svyatoslav N. Fyodorov in the early 1970s. There are two different stories as to how Fyodorov came to use radial keratotomy successfully. One story tells of a boy whose eyeglasses shattered and left tiny fragments of glass embedded in his cornea. Another story tells of a pilot with similar accidental cuts in his cornea. In either (or both) cases, Fyodorov noticed that when the cuts had healed, the patient's previously poor vision had improved because the cornea had been "flattened" by the accidental cuts. Fyodorov soon began to perform cornea surgeries regularly by 1974, and by the late 1970s, his new technique had become known around the world. In 1978, Leo Bores became the first to perform a radial keratotomy in the United States and soon after began training others.

Radial keratotomy was found to improve nearsightedness because it flattened the central part of the cornea by making cuts in its sides. The length, depth, and number of cuts was usually different in each case, depending on the patient's condition, age, and the curve of the cornea. This flattening of the cornea brought the focal point of the eye closer to the retina and improved distance vision. The surgery was performed using a highly precise diamond-tipped or sapphire-tipped scalpel (blade) that is set to a particular depth. This surgery is usually quick, generally painless, and its recovery period short. However, it sometimes resulted in irregular healing or infection. Others have experienced what is called "variable vision" in the course of a day, and sometimes scarring would result in blurred vision.

New laser surgery

Although radial keratotomy is still performed and even recommended for certain cases, most eye doctors now recommend it be replaced by laser surgery. Laser vision correction, now known as LASIK surgery (for LASer In situ Keratmileusis), is the newest and usually best form of radial keratotomy. Instead of using a knife to makes slits in the cornea, the surgeon reshapes the cornea using a process called "photoablation" (pronounced foe-toe-ab-LAY-shun). This process uses an intense beam of ultraviolet laser light that is precisely controlled. With it, the surgeon stimulates the molecules in the cornea to the point where certain ones break apart and vaporize. The tissue that is disappearing is actually no more than one five hundredth the thickness of a human hair. What is remarkable about this procedure is that the tissue around and even underneath is not at all affected.

Doctors use a computer to perform laser vision correction surgery and program its software according to a number of variables since each patient is different. Today's laser vision correction has become quicker, cheaper, and safer than ever. Modern LASIK has rapidly become the procedure of choice for most surgeons who recommend it because it produces better results with less discomfort in a quicker period of time. Overall, the older, scalpel-based radial keratotomy has increasingly been replaced by the newer laser-based surgery. Radial keratotomy was an important step in the evolution of vision correction surgery.

[*See also* **Eye**]

Radial keratotomy scars on the human eye. (*Reproduced by permission of Phototake.*)

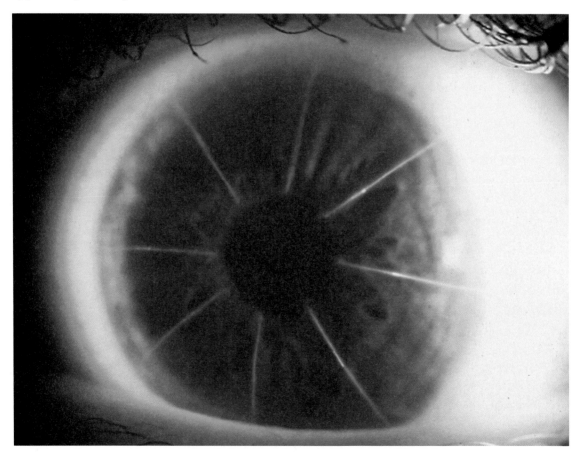

Radiation

The word radiation comes from a Latin term that means "ray of light." It is used in a general sense to cover all forms of energy that travel through space from one place to another as "rays." Radiation may occur in the form of a spray of subatomic particles, like miniature bullets from a machine gun, or in the form of electromagnetic waves. Subatomic particles are the basic units of matter and energy (electrons, neutrons, protons, neutrinos, and positrons), which are even smaller than atoms. Electromagnetic waves are a form of energy that includes light itself, as well as other forms of energy such as X rays, gamma rays, radio waves, and radar.

In addition, the word radiation is sometimes used to describe the transfer of heat from a hot object to a cooler one that is not touching the first object. The hot object is said to radiate heat. You can feel the heat on your face when standing near a red-hot furnace, even if there is no movement of hot air between the furnace and you. What you feel is infrared radiation, a form of electromagnetic energy that we experience as heat.

When some people hear the word radiation, they think of the radiation that comes from radioactive materials. This radiation consists of both particles and electromagnetic waves. Both forms of radiation can be harmful because they carry a great deal of energy. When they come into contact with atoms, they tend to tear the atoms apart by removing electrons from them. This damage to atoms may cause materials to undergo changes that can be harmful or damaging. For example, plastics exposed to radiation from radioactive sources can become very brittle. (This effect can be contrasted to the passage of light and some other forms of electromagnetic radiation. These forms of energy generally have no lasting effect on a material. For example, a piece of clear plastic is not damaged when light passes through it.)

High energy radiation, such as that of X rays and gamma rays, is also called ionizing radiation, a name that comes from the ability of the radiation to remove electrons from atoms. The particles left behind when electrons are removed are called ions. Ionizing radiation can cause serious damage to both living and nonliving materials.

Electromagnetic radiation

Electromagnetic radiation travels in the form of waves moving in straight lines at a speed of about 186,282 miles (299,727 kilometers) per second. That speed is correct when electromagnetic radiation travels through a vacuum. When it passes through a transparent substance such as glass, water, or air, the speed decreases. However, the velocity of electromagnetic waves, also known as the speed of light in a vacuum, is a fundamental constant of nature. That is, it cannot be changed by humans or, presumably, by anything else. (The term velocity refers both to the speed with which an object is moving and to the direction in which it is moving.)

Electromagnetic radiation can have a variety of energies. Because it travels in the form of waves, the energies are often expressed in terms of wavelengths. The higher the energy of a wave, the shorter its wavelength. The wavelengths of known electromagnetic radiation range from less than 10^{-10} centimeter for the highest energies up to millions of centimeters (tens of miles) for the lowest energies.

The energy of a wave can also be expressed by stating its frequency. The frequency of a wave is defined as the number of wave crests (or troughs; pronounced trawfs) that pass a given point per second. This is usually measured in vibrations or cycles per second. Scientists call one cycle per second a hertz, abbreviated Hz. Known electromagnetic radiations range in frequency from a few Hz for the lowest energies up to more than 10^{20} Hz for the highest.

Particulate radiation

Sprays or streams of invisibly small particles are often referred to as particulate radiation because they carry energy along with them as they fly through space. They may be produced deliberately in machines, such as particle accelerators (atom-smashers), or they may be emitted spontaneously from radioactive materials. Alpha particles and beta particles are emitted by radioactive materials, while beams of electrons, protons, mesons, neutrons, ions, and even whole atoms and molecules can be produced in particle accelerators (used to study subatomic particles and other matter), nuclear reactors (used to control the energy released by nuclear reactions), and other kinds of laboratory apparatus.

The only particulate radiation that might be encountered outside of a laboratory are alpha and beta particles emitted by naturally occurring radioactive materials. Both alpha particles and beta particles are charged subatomic particles. An alpha particle is the nucleus of a helium atom. It has an electric charge of +2 and a mass of 4 atomic mass units (amu). A beta particle is an electron. It has a charge of −1 and a mass of about 0.0055 amu.

Because of their electric charges, both alpha and beta particles attract or repel electrons in the atoms of any material through which they pass, thereby ionizing those atoms. If enough of these ionized atoms happen to be parts of essential molecules in a human body, the body's chemistry can be seriously disrupted, resulting in health problems.

Radiation and health

Large doses of any kind of radiation, ionizing or not, can be dangerous. Too much sunlight, for example, can damage a person's eyes or skin. Lasers can deliver such intense beams of light that they can burn through metal—not to mention human flesh. Microwaves in ovens are at such high levels they cook meats and vegetables.

On the other hand, small amounts of any kind of radiation are generally thought to be harmless. Even low doses of ionizing radiation from radioactive materials is probably not dangerous. The latter fact is of special importance because radioactive materials occur in small concentrations all around us.

[*See also* **Electromagnetic field; Nuclear medicine; Radioactive tracers; Radioactivity; Subatomic particles; X rays**]

Radiation exposure

The term radiation exposure refers to any occasion on which a human or other animal or a plant has been placed in the presence of radiation from a radioactive source. For example, scientists have learned that the radioactive element radon is present in the basements of some homes and office buildings. Radon gas gives off radiation that can cause damage to human cells. Anyone living in a home or working in an office where radon is present runs some risk of being exposed to the radiation from this element.

The term radiation itself refers both to high speed subatomic particles, such as streams of alpha particles or beta particles, and to electromagnetic radiation. Electromagnetic radiation is a type of energy that travels in waves and includes such forms as X rays, gamma rays, ultraviolet radiation, infrared radiation, and visible light. Concerns about radiation exposure are, however, limited almost exclusively to effects caused by radiation emitted by radioactive materials: alpha and beta particles and gamma rays.

Sources of radiation

Radiation comes from both natural and human sources. Many elements exist in one or more radioactive forms. The most common of these is an isotope known as potassium 40. Isotopes are forms of an element

Words to Know

Background radiation: The natural level of radiation present on Earth at all times.

Ionization: The process by which atoms or molecules lose electrons and become positively charged particles.

Radiation: Energy transmitted in the form of electromagnetic waves or subatomic particles.

Radiation detectors: Instruments that are able to sense and relay information about the presence of radiation.

Radiation sickness: A term used to describe a variety of symptoms that develop when a person is exposed to radiation.

Radioactivity: The property possessed by some elements of spontaneously emitting energy in the form of particles or waves by disintegration of their atomic nuclei.

Subatomic particle: Basic unit of matter and energy (proton, neutron, electron, neutrino, and positron) smaller than an atom.

that differ from each other in the structure of their nuclei. Other radioactive isotopes found in nature include hydrogen 3, carbon 14, chlorine 39, lead 212, radium 226, and uranium 235 and 238.

Humans and other organisms cannot escape exposure to radiation from these radioactive sources. They constitute a normal radiation, called background radiation, that is simply part of existing on Earth. Although some harmful effects can be produced by exposure to natural background radiation, those effects are relatively minor and, in most cases, not even measurable.

Human activities have added to normal background radiation over the past half century. When nuclear weapons are exploded, for example, they release radioactive isotopes into the atmosphere. As these radioactive isotopes are spread around the world by prevailing winds, they come into contact with humans and other organisms.

Nuclear power plants are also a potential source of radiation. Such plants are normally constructed with very high levels of safety in mind, and there is little or no evidence that humans are at risk as the result of the normal operation of a nuclear power plant. On those rare occasions when damage occurs to a nuclear power plant, however, that situation can change dramatically. Accidents at the Three Mile Island Plant in Pennsylvania in 1979 and at the Chernobyl Plant outside Kiev in Ukraine in 1986, for example, caused the release of substantial amounts of radiation to the areas surrounding the plants. In both cases, people were either injured or killed as a result of the release of radiation.

Effects of radiation

The harmful effects of exposure to radiation are due largely to its ionizing effects. Atoms and molecules contain electrons that can be

A radiation victim in Rongelap, an atoll in the Marshall Islands in the western Pacific. *(Reproduced by permission of Greenpeace Photos.)*

removed from their orbits rather easily. For example, if a beta particle passes through an atom, it has the ability to repel any electrons in its path, ejecting them from the atom.

The bonds that hold atoms together in molecules are made of electrons. A molecule of water, for example, consists of oxygen and hydrogen atoms held together by electrons. If radiation passes through or very near a molecule of water, it may cause electrons to be ejected from the molecule. When that happens, the water molecule may fall apart. The same process occurs in any kind of molecule, including proteins, lipids, nucleic acids, and carbohydrates, the molecules of which living organisms are constructed.

Damage to molecules of this kind can have two general effects. First, when essential molecules are destroyed, an organism is no longer able to carry on all the normal functions it needs in order to stay alive and to function properly. A person, for example, may become sick if essential enzymes (substances that speed up chemical reactions) in his or her body are destroyed.

Some of the symptoms of radiation sickness include actual burns to the skin, nausea, vomiting, and diarrhea. The specific effects observed depend on the kind of radiation to which the person was exposed and the length of exposure. For example, a person exposed to low doses of radiation may experience some of the least severe symptoms of radiation sickness and then get better. A person exposed to higher doses of radiation may become seriously ill and even die.

Exposure to radiation can have long-term effects as well. These effects include the development of various kinds of cancer, leukemia being one of the most common types. Damage to a person's deoxyribonucleic acid (DNA) can also cause reproductive defects, such as children who are born deformed, blind, mentally impaired, or with other physical or mental challenges. (DNA is a complex molecule in the nucleus of cells that stores and transmits genetic information.)

Radiation detectors

All forms of radiation are invisible. You could stand in an area being flooded with life-threatening levels of alpha and beta particles and gamma rays, and you would never be able to tell. It is for this reason that anyone who works in an area where radioactivity is to be expected must be provided with radiation detectors. A radiation detector is an instrument that is able to sense and report on the presence of radiation.

Many kinds of radiation detectors are now available. One of the most common of these is the film badge. A film badge consists of a piece of photographic film wrapped in black paper behind the badge. When radiation passes through the badge, it exposes the photographic film. The film is removed from the badge at regular intervals and developed. The amount of radiation received by the wearer of the badge can then easily be determined by the amount of fogging on the photographic film.

A Geiger counter, another type of radiation detector, is a cylindrical glass tube with a thin wire down the middle. When radiation passes through the tube, it ionizes the gas inside the tube. The ions formed travel to the central wire where they initiate an electrical current through the wire. The wire is connected with an audible signal or a visual display. The clicking sound made or the light produced in the Geiger counter is an indication of the amount of radiation passing through the tube.

Cloud chambers and bubble chambers provide a visual display of radiation. When radiation passes through a cloud chamber, it causes moisture in the chamber to condense in much the same way a contrail (cloud) forms when a jet airplane passes through the sky. In a bubble chamber, it is a string of bubbles rather than a string of water droplets that forms. In either case, the path of the radiation and even the form of the radiation can be traced by the water droplets or bubbles formed in one of these devices.

[*See also* **Mutation; Radiation; Radioactivity**]

A handheld Geiger counter. *(Reproduced by permission of Photo Researchers, Inc.)*

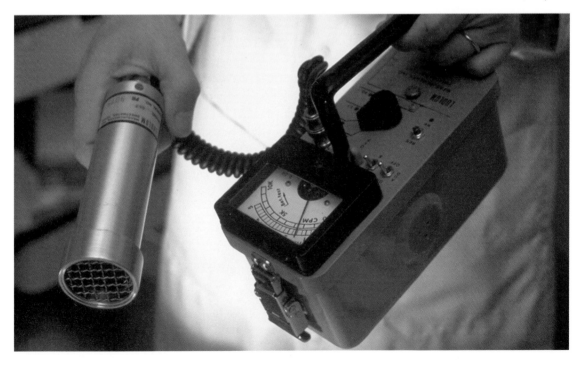

Radio

Radio is the technology that allows information to be transmitted and received over radio waves. Radio makes it possible to establish wireless two-way communication between individual pairs of transmitters/receivers and it is used for one-way broadcasts to many receivers. Radio signals can carry speech, music, or digitally encoded entertainment. Radio waves occur naturally in space or can be created by people. They are a long-wave form of electromagnetic radiation, or radiation that transmits energy through the interaction of electricity and magnetism.

The history of radio

In the nineteenth century, Scottish physicist James Clerk Maxwell (1831–1879) developed a mathematical theory proving that magnetism and electricity were related. His theory linking the two forces became known as the electromagnetic theory. He predicted that light is only one type of electromagnetic radiation and that wavelengths should exist below infrared (those situated outside the visible spectrum at the red or long-wavelength end) and above ultraviolet (situated outside the visible spectrum at the violet or short-wavelength end). In the 1880s, German physicist Heinrich Hertz (1857–1894) discovered extremely long-wavelength radio waves, proving Maxwell's theory.

Italian physicist and engineer Guglielmo Marconi (1874–1937), fascinated with Hertz's discovery of radio waves, built his first crude radio transmitter and receiver in 1895. In 1901, using his "wireless" (as radio was called then), he sent the first message via signals similar to Morse code (which uses dots and dashes for letters and numbers) across the Atlantic Ocean. In the succeeding years, other scientists improved on Marconi's invention, and it eventually became possible to send voice signals by radio waves.

Radio broadcasting as we know it today began in 1920. Station KDKA in Pittsburgh, Pennsylvania, made the announcement to the few people who owned radio receivers that Warren G. Harding had been elected president of the United States. Within a few years, many homes had radio receivers and several radio stations scheduled regular programming.

Radio waves and frequencies

Although turning on a radio produces sound, radio waves themselves cannot be "heard" and have nothing to do with sound waves. While sound waves are a vibration of the air, radio waves are electromagnetic and a part of the light spectrum. Radio waves travel at a speed of 186,282 miles

Words to Know

Carrier wave: Radio signal with superimposed information.

Electromagnetic radiation: Radiation that transmits energy through the interaction of electricity and magnetism.

Infrared radiation: Electromagnetic radiation of a wavelength shorter than radio waves but longer than visible light that takes the form of heat.

Modulation: Process by which a characteristic of radio waves, such as amplitude or frequency, is changed to make the waves correspond to a signal or information that is being transmitted.

Ultraviolet radiation: Electromagnetic radiation of a wavelength just shorter than the violet end of the visible light spectrum.

Wavelength: The distance between two peaks in any wave.

(299,727 kilometers) per second—the speed of light. Radio waves travel through the air, surrounding us with vibrations that can only be detected through a radio receiver.

Radio programs begin as sound waves, which microphones change into electrical signals. From the antenna atop the radio station, the electrical signals are broadcast as electromagnetic waves. The receiver picks up the waves in the air, electrically amplifies (enlarges) them, and converts them back into sound through the speaker of the radio in your home.

Although radio waves from many stations surround us all the time, the radio does not receive them all at the same time because the stations broadcast at different frequencies. A frequency is the number of times per second that radio waves vibrate. The numbers on a radio dial represent the frequencies used by radio stations in your area. For example, if the dial is set at 96, the radio signal you hear is broadcasted at 960 kilocycles, or 960,000 cycles per second.

Modulation

A radio signal alone, without information (speech, music) added to it, is called a carrier wave. Adding information to a carrier signal is a process called modulation. The simplest modulation method is to vary the strength of the signal. The result is called amplitude modulation, or AM.

The method that varies the signal's frequency is known as frequency modulation, or FM. AM radio waves are about 1,000 feet (1,600 kilometers) in wavelength, while FM radio waves are only a few feet in wavelength. Broadcasts on AM radio stations can often be heard for hundreds of miles, especially at night when electromagnetic interference is minimal. Broadcasts on FM stations do not travel such a distance, but they have better sound quality and are not affected by lightning-caused static that often plagues AM broadcasts.

[*See also* **Electromagnetic spectrum**]

Radio towers on Elden Mountain above Flagstaff, Arizona. The size of each transmitting antenna matches the wavelength of the signal it transmits. *(Reproduced by permission of The Stock Market.)*

Radioactive tracers

Radioactive tracers are substances that contain a radioactive atom to allow easier detection and measurement. (Radioactivity is the property possessed by some elements of spontaneously emitting energy in the form of particles or waves by disintegration of their atomic nuclei.) For example, it is possible to make a molecule of water in which one of the two hydrogen atoms is a radioactive tritium (hydrogen-3) atom. This molecule behaves in almost the same way as a normal molecule of water. The main difference between the tracer molecule containing tritium and the normal molecule is that the tracer molecule continually gives off radiation that can be detected with a Geiger counter or some other type of radiation-detection instrument.

One application for the tracer molecule described above would be to monitor plant growth by watering plants with it. The plants would take up the water and use it in leaves, roots, stems, flowers, and other parts in the same way it does with normal water. In this case, however, it would be possible to find out how fast the water moves into any one part of the plant. One would simply pass a Geiger counter over the plant at regular intervals and see where the water has gone.

Applications

Industry and research. Radioactive tracers have applications in medicine, industry, agriculture, research, and many other fields of science and technology. For example, a number of different oil companies may take turns using the same pipeline to ship their products from the oil fields to their refineries. How do companies A, B, and C all know when their oil is passing through the pipeline? One way to solve that problem is to add a radioactive tracer to the oil. Each company would be assigned a different tracer. A technician at the receiving end of the pipeline can use a Geiger counter to make note of changes in radiation observed in the incoming oil. Such a change would indicate that oil for a different company was being received.

Another application of tracers might be in scientific research on plant nutrition. Suppose that a scientist wants to find out how plants use some nutrient such as phosphorus. The scientist could feed a group of plants fertilizer that contains radioactive phosphorus. As the plant grows, the location of the phosphorus could be detected by use of a Geiger counter. Another way to trace the movement of the phosphorus would be to place a piece of photographic film against the plant. Radiation from the phosphorus tracer would expose the film, in effect taking its own picture of its role in plant growth.

Medical applications. Some of the most interesting and valuable applications of radioactive tracers have been in the field of medicine. For example, when a person ingests (takes into the body) the element iodine, that element goes largely to the thyroid gland located at the base of the throat. There the iodine is used in the production of various hormones (chemical messengers) that control essential body functions such as the rate of metabolism (energy production and use).

Suppose that a physician suspects that a person's thyroid gland is not functioning properly. To investigate that possibility, the patient can be given a glass of water containing sodium iodide (similar to sodium chloride, or table salt). The iodine in the sodium iodide is radioactive. As the patient's body takes up the sodium iodide, the path of the compound through the body can be traced by means of a Geiger counter or some other detection device. The physician can determine whether the rate and location of uptake is normal or abnormal and, from that information, can diagnose any problems with the patient's thyroid gland.

[*See also* **Isotope; Nuclear medicine; Radioactivity**]

Radioactivity

Radioactivity is the emission of radiation by unstable nuclei. That radiation may exist in the form of subatomic particles (primarily alpha and beta particles) or in the form of energy (primarily gamma rays).

Radioactivity was discovered accidentally in 1896 by French physicist Henri Becquerel (1852–1908). In the decades that followed Becquerel's discovery, research on radioactivity produced revolutionary breakthroughs in our understanding of the nature of matter and led to a number of important practical applications. These applications include a host of new devices and techniques ranging from nuclear weapons and nuclear power plants to medical techniques that can be used for diagnosing and treating serious diseases.

Stable and unstable nuclei

The nucleus of all atoms (with the exception of hydrogen) contains one or more protons and one or more neutrons. The nucleus of most car-

Words to Know

Alpha particle: The nucleus of a helium atom, consisting of two protons and two neutrons.

Beta particle: An electron emitted by an atomic nucleus.

Gamma ray: A high-energy form of electromagnetic radiation.

Isotopes: Two or more forms of an element with the same number of protons but different numbers of neutrons in their atomic nuclei.

Nucleus (atomic): The core of an atom, usually consisting of one or more protons and neutrons.

Radioactive decay: The process by which an atomic nucleus gives off radiation and changes into a new nucleus.

Radioactive family: A group of radioactive isotopes in which the decay of one isotope leads to the formation of another radioactive isotope.

Stable nucleus: An atomic nucleus that does not undergo any changes spontaneously.

Subatomic particle: Basic unit of matter and energy (proton, neutron, electron, neutrino, and positron) smaller than an atom.

Unstable nucleus: An atomic nucleus that undergoes some internal change spontaneously.

bon atoms, for instance, contains six protons and six neutrons. In most cases, the nuclei of atoms are stable; that is, they do not undergo changes on their own. A carbon nucleus will look exactly the same a hundred years from now (or a million years from now) as it does today.

But some nuclei are unstable. An unstable nucleus is one that undergoes some internal change spontaneously. In this change, the nucleus gives off a subatomic particle, or a burst of energy, or both. As an example, an isotope of carbon, carbon-14, has a nucleus consisting of six protons and eight (rather than six) neutrons. A nucleus that gives off a particle or energy is said to undergo radioactive decay, or just decay.

Scientists are not entirely clear as to what makes a nucleus unstable. It seems that some nuclei contain an excess number of protons or neutrons or an excess amount of energy. These nuclei restore what must for them be a proper balance of protons, neutrons, and energy by giving off a subatomic particle or a burst of energy.

In this process, the nucleus changes its composition and may actually become a different nucleus entirely. For example, in its attempt to achieve stability, a carbon-14 nucleus gives off a beta particle. After the carbon-14 nucleus has lost the beta particle, it consists of seven protons and seven neutrons. But a nucleus consisting of seven protons and seven neutrons is no longer a carbon nucleus. It is now the nucleus of a nitrogen atom. By giving off a beta particle, the carbon-14 atom has changed into a nitrogen atom.

Types of radiation

The forms of radiation most commonly emitted by a radioactive nucleus are called alpha particles, beta particles, and gamma rays. An alpha particle is the nucleus of a helium atom. It consists of two protons and two neutrons. Consider the case of a radium-226 atom. The nucleus of a radium-226 atom consists of 88 protons and 138 neutrons. If that nucleus gives off an alpha particle, it must lose the two protons and two neutrons of which the alpha particle is made. After emission of the alpha particle, the remaining nucleus contains only 86 protons (88 − 2) and 136 neutrons (138 − 2). This nucleus is the nucleus of a radon atom, not a radium atom. By emitting an alpha particle, the radium-226 atom has changed into an atom of radon.

The emission of beta particles from nuclei was a source of confusion for scientists for many years. A beta particle is an electron. The problem is that electrons do not exist in the nuclei of atoms. They can be found outside the nucleus but not within it. How is it possible, then, for an unstable nucleus to give off a beta particle (electron)?

The answer is that the beta particle is produced when a neutron inside the atomic nucleus breaks apart to form a proton and an electron:

$$\text{neutron} \rightarrow \text{proton} + \text{electron}$$

Recall that a proton carries a single positive charge and the electron a single negative charge. That means that a neutron, which carries no electrical charge at all, can break apart to form two new particles (a proton and an electron) whose electrical charges add up to make zero.

Think back to the example of carbon-14, mentioned earlier. A carbon-14 nucleus decays by giving off a beta particle. That means that one neutron in the carbon-14 nucleus breaks apart to form a proton and an electron. The electron is given off as a beta ray, and the proton remains behind in the nucleus. The new nucleus contains seven protons (its original six plus one new proton) and seven neutrons (its original eight reduced by the breakdown of one).

The loss of an alpha particle or a beta particle from an unstable nucleus is often accompanied by the loss of a gamma ray. A gamma ray is a form of high-energy radiation. It is similar to an X ray but of somewhat greater energy. Some unstable nuclei can decay by the emission of gamma rays only. When they have lost the energy carried away by the gamma rays, they become stable.

Natural and synthetic radioactivity

Many radioactive elements occur in nature. In fact, all of the elements heavier than bismuth (atomic number 83) are radioactive. They have no stable isotopes.

The heaviest of the radioactive elements are involved in sequences known as radioactive families. A radioactive family is a group of elements in which the decay of one radioactive element produces another element that is also radioactive. As an example, the parent isotope of one radioactive family is uranium-238. When uranium-238 decays, it forms thorium-234. But thorium-234 is also radioactive. When it decays, it forms protactinium-234. Protactinium-234, in turn, is also radioactive and decays to form uranium-234. The process continues for another eleven steps. Finally, the isotope polonium-210 decays to form lead-206, which is stable.

Many lighter elements also have radioactive isotopes. Some examples include hydrogen-3, carbon-14, potassium-40, and tellurium-123.

Radioactive isotopes can also be made artificially. The usual process is to bombard a stable nucleus with protons, neutrons, alpha particles, or other subatomic particles. The bombardment process can be accomplished with particle accelerators (atom-smashers) or in nuclear reactors. When one of the bombarding particles (bullets) hits a stable nucleus, it may cause that nucleus to become unstable and, therefore, turn radioactive.

[*See also* **Atom; Isotope; Nuclear fission; Nuclear fusion; Nuclear medicine; Nuclear power; Subatomic particles; X rays**]

Radio astronomy

Matter in the universe emits radiation (energy) from all parts of the electromagnetic spectrum, the range of wavelengths produced by the interaction of electricity and magnetism. The electromagnetic spectrum includes

Words to Know

Big bang theory: Theory that explains the beginning of the universe as a tremendous explosion from a single point that occurred 12 to 15 billion years ago.

Electromagnetic radiation: Radiation that transmits energy through the interaction of electricity and magnetism.

Gamma rays: Short-wavelength, high-energy radiation formed either by the decay of radioactive elements or by nuclear reactions.

Infrared radiation: Electromagnetic radiation of a wavelength shorter than radio waves but longer than visible light that takes the form of heat.

Pulsars: Rapidly spinning, blinking neutron stars.

Quasars: Extremely bright, starlike sources of radio waves that are the oldest known objects in the universe.

Radio waves: Longest form of electromagnetic radiation, measuring up to 6 miles from peak to peak.

Ultraviolet radiation: Electromagnetic radiation (energy) of a wavelength just shorter than the violet (shortest wavelength) end of the visible light spectrum.

Wavelength: The distance between two peaks in any wave.

X rays: Electromagnetic radiation of a wavelength just shorter than ultraviolet radiation but longer than gamma rays that can penetrate solids and produce an electrical charge in gases.

light waves, radio waves, infrared radiation, ultraviolet radiation, X rays, and gamma rays.

Radio astronomy is the study of celestial objects by means of the radio waves they emit. Radio waves are the longest form of electromagnetic radiation. Some of these waves measure up to 6 miles (more than 9 kilometers) from peak to peak. Objects that appear very dim or are invisible to our eye may have very strong radio waves.

In some respects, radio waves are an even better tool for astronomical observation than light waves. Light waves are blocked out by clouds, dust, and other materials in Earth's atmosphere. Light waves from distant objects are also invisible during daylight because light from the Sun is so bright that the less intense light waves from more distant objects cannot be seen. Radio waves, however, can be detected as easily during the day as they can at night.

Origins of radio astronomy

No one individual can be given complete credit for the development of radio astronomy. However, an important pioneer in the field was Karl Jansky, a scientist employed at the Bell Telephone Laboratories in Murray Hill, New Jersey. In the early 1930s, Jansky was working on the problem of noise sources that might interfere with the transmission of shortwave radio signals. During his research, Jansky discovered that his instruments picked up static every day at about the same time and in about the same part of the sky. It was later discovered that the source of this static was the center of the Milky Way galaxy.

Grote Reber, an amateur radio enthusiast in Wheaton, Illinois, took it upon himself to begin examining the radio signals from space. In 1937, he built the world's first radio dish—out of rafters, galvanized sheet metal, and auto parts—to collect radio signals in his back yard. He mounted a receiver above the dish. Reber produced the first radio maps of the sky,

Very large array (VLA) radio telescopes in Socorra, New Mexico. *(Reproduced by permission of JLM Visuals.)*

discovering points where strong radio signals were being emitted. He worked virtually alone until the end of World War II (1939–45), when scientists began adapting radar tracking devices for use as radio telescopes.

What radio astronomy has revealed

Scientists have found that radio signals come from everywhere. Our knowledge of nearly every object in the cosmos has been improved by the use of radio telescopes. Radio astronomy has amassed an incredible amount of information, much of it surprising and unexpected.

The eta Carinae nebula as seen by visible light (bottom), X rays (top left), and radio waves (right). Each shows a different image of the nebula. (Reproduced by permission of National Aeronautics and Space Administration.)

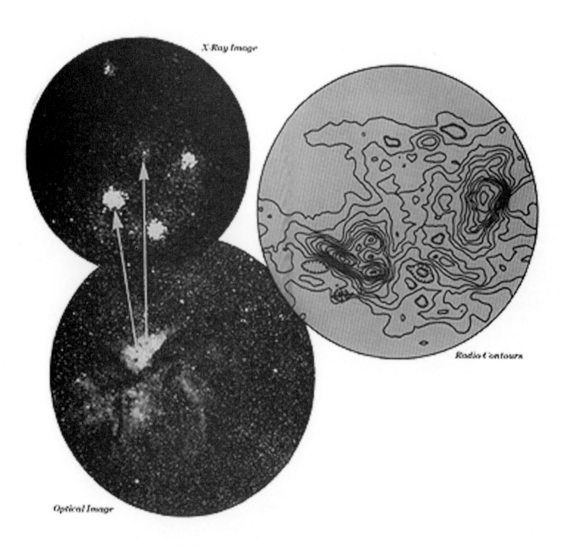

X-Ray Image

Radio Contours

Optical Image

In 1955, astrophysicists detected radio bursts coming from Jupiter. Next to the Sun, this planet is the strongest source of radio waves in the solar system. Around this time, Dutch astronomer Jan Oort used a radio telescope to map the spiral structure of the Milky Way galaxy. In 1960, several small but intense radio sources were discovered that did not fit into any previously known classification. They were called quasi-stellar radio sources. Further investigation revealed them to be quasars, the most distant and therefore the oldest celestial objects known. And in the late 1960s, English astronomers Antony Hewish and Jocelyn Bell Burnell detected the first pulsar (neutron star), a strong radio source in the core of the Crab Nebula.

Evidence of the big bang. In 1964, radio astronomers found very compelling evidence in support of the big bang theory of how the universe began. Americans Arno Penzias and Robert Wilson discovered a constant background noise that seemed to come from every direction in the sky. Further investigation revealed this noise to be radiation (now called cosmic microwave background) that had a temperature of −465°F (−276°C). This corresponded to the predicted temperature to which radiation left over from the formation of the universe 12 to 15 billion years ago would have cooled by the present.

Today astronomers use radio astronomy and other sophisticated methods including gamma ray, infrared, and X-ray astronomy to examine the cosmos. The largest single radio telescope dish presently in operation, with a diameter of 1,000 feet (305 meters), is in Arecibo, Puerto Rico.

[*See also* **Galaxy; Pulsar; Quasar; Telescope**]

Radiology

Radiology is a branch of medical science in which various forms of radiant energy are used to diagnose and treat disorders and diseases. For nearly 80 years, radiology was based primarily on the use of X rays. Since the 1970s, however, several new imaging techniques have been developed. Some, like computed tomography, makes use of X rays along with other technology, such as computer technology. Others, like ultrasound and magnetic resonance imaging, use forms of radiant energy other than X rays.

Radiant energy

The term radiant energy refers to any form of electromagnetic energy, such as cosmic rays, gamma rays, X rays, infrared radiation, visible

▼ Words to Know

Angiography: Imaging of a blood vessel by injecting a radiopaque substance in the bloodstream and exposing the body to X rays.

Computerized axial tomography (CAT): A body imaging technique in which X-ray photographs taken from a number of angles are combined by means of a computer program.

Diagnosis: Identification of a disease or disorder.

Electromagnetic radiation: Radiation that transmits energy through the interaction of electricity and magnetism.

Imaging: The process by which a "picture" is taken of the interior of a body.

Myelography: Imaging of the spinal code by radiologic techniques.

Positron emission tomography (PET): A radiologic imaging technique that makes use of photographs produced by radiation given off by radioactive materials injected into a person's body.

Radiant energy: Any form of electromagnetic energy.

Radiation therapy: The use of X rays or other radioactive substances to treat disease.

Radiopaque: Any substance through which X rays cannot pass.

Ultrasound: A form of energy that consists of waves traveling with frequencies higher than can be heard by humans; also, a technique for imaging the human body and other objects using ultrasound energy.

X rays: Electromagnetic radiation of a wavelength just shorter than ultraviolet radiation but longer than gamma rays that can penetrate solids.

light, ultraviolet radiation, radar, radio waves, and microwaves. These forms of energy are classified together because they all travel by means of waves. They differ from each other only in their frequencies (the number of times per second that waves vibrate) and wavelengths (the distance between two peaks in any wave).

Various forms of radiant energy interact with matter in different ways. For example, visible light does not pass through most forms of matter. If you hold a sheet of paper between yourself and a friend, you will not be able to see your friend. Light waves from the friend are not able to pass through the paper.

Forms of radiant energy with higher frequencies than visible light are able to penetrate matter better than does visible light. For example, if you were to place a sheet of paper between yourself and an X-ray machine, X rays would be able to pass through the paper and to strike your body.

X rays for diagnosis

The ability of X rays to pass through matter makes them useful as a diagnostic tool to identify a disease or disorder. As an example, suppose that a doctor believes that a child has broken a bone in her arm. In order to confirm this diagnosis, the doctor may take an X ray of the child's arm. In this process, the child's arm is placed beneath a machine that emits X rays. Those X rays pass through flesh in the arm without being stopped. But the X rays are not able to pass through bone as easily. A photographic plate placed beneath the child's arm "takes a picture" of X rays that have passed through the arm. Fleshy parts of the arm show up as exposed areas, while bone shows up as unexposed areas. A doctor can look at the photograph produced and determine whether the bone is solid or has been broken. Making pictures of the interior of a person's body by a process such as this is known as imaging.

Over the years, radiologists have developed more sophisticated ways of using X rays for diagnosis. For example, regions of the body in which tissue is more dense than in other regions can be detected by X-ray imaging. The presence of such dense spots may indicate the presence of a tumor or some other abnormal structure.

Radiologists also make use of substances through which X rays cannot pass, substances that are called radiopaque. Suppose that a radiopaque substance is injected into a person's bloodstream and an X ray made of the person's arm. This process is known as angiography. The radiopaque substance in the bloodstream will show up on the X-ray photograph and allow a doctor to determine the presence of abnormalities in veins, arteries, or other parts of the circulatory system.

Another form of angiography is called myelography. In this process, a radiopaque substance is injected in the membrane covering the spine, and an X-ray photograph is taken. The resulting image can be used to diagnose problems with the spine.

Computers and radiology

In recent decades, radiologists have developed a variety of techniques in which the powers of X rays and computers have been brought together. The earliest of these techniques was computerized axial tomography

(CAT). In computerized axial tomography, an X-ray machine is rotated around a person's body. Pictures are taken of some specific part of the body from many different angles. Those pictures are then put together by a computer to provide a three-dimensional image of the body part being studied.

A variation of the CAT technique is known as positron emission tomography (PET). In this technique, a radioactive material is injected into a person's body. That radioactive material emits positrons (positive electrons) and gamma rays. A scanner "reads" the gamma rays in much the same ways that X rays are scanned in a CAT machine. However, the specific radioactive material used in the process can be chosen to produce much finer images than are available with a CAT scan. Another variation of the PET process is called single photon emission computerized tomography (SPECT).

One of the first techniques used in radiology not based on X rays was ultrasound. Ultrasound is a form of energy that consists of waves

The viewing room of a Magnetic Resonance Imaging (MRI) system. *(Reproduced by permission of FPG International LLC.)*

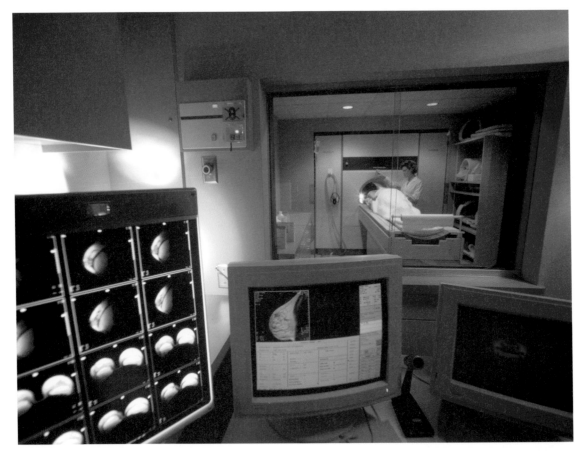

traveling with frequencies higher than can be heard by humans. Ultrasound has some of the same abilities to pass through human tissue as do X rays. One of the first uses of ultrasound was to detect defects in metallic structures. Later, it became a common and powerful tool for imaging a fetus while it is still in the uterus (womb). In this procedure, a sound transmitter is used to send waves into the pregnant woman's body from various angles. As these waves bounce back off the uterus and the fetus, they are recorded both on a television screen and in a photograph. With this technology, a physician can recognize problems that may exist within the fetus or the pregnant woman's uterus.

Therapeutic applications

Radiological techniques can also be used for therapeutic purposes, methods used to treat diseases and disorders. The use of radiology for therapy depends on the fact that X rays kill living cells. Under normal circumstances, this fact provides a good reason for people to avoid coming into contact with X rays. The destruction of healthy cells by X rays is, in fact, one of the ways in which cancers may develop.

This same fact, however, provides the basis for treating cancer. Cancer is a disease characterized by the rapid, out-of-control growth of cells. Suppose that a person has been diagnosed with cancer of the spleen, for example. That diagnosis means that cells in the spleen have begun to grow much more rapidly than normal. It follows that one way to treat this condition is to bombard the spleen with X rays. Since the cancer cells are the cells growing most rapidly, they are most likely to be the cells killed by the X rays. The fact that healthy cells are also killed in this process is shown by the side-effects of radiation therapy: loss of hair, nausea, loss of weight, among others. In fact, the success of radiation therapy depends to some extent on the physician's ability to focus the cell-killing X rays on cancer cells and to protect healthy cells from those same X rays.

[See also **X rays**]

Rain forest

Rain forests are ecosystems characterized by high annual precipitation and an abundance of many large trees, generally of very old age. (An ecosystem is an ecological community, or the plants, animals, and microorganisms in a region considered together with their environment.) Rain forests can be found in both tropical and temperate regions. (Temperate regions

▼ Words to Know

Biomass: The sum total of living and once-living matter contained within a given geographic area.

Biodiversity: The wide range of organisms—plants and animals—that exist within any geographical location.

Canopy: The "covering" of a forest, consisting of the highest level of tree branches and foliage in the forest.

Ecosystem: An ecological community, including plants, animals, and microorganisms, considered together with their environment.

Old-growth forest: A mature forest, characterized by great age and many large and very old trees, with a complex physical structure.

Temperate: Mild or moderate.

Tropical: Characteristic of a region or climate that is frost free with temperatures high enough to support—with adequate precipitation—plant growth year round.

have mild or moderate climates; tropical regions have high enough temperatures and enough rain to support plant growth year round.) Rain forests require a humid climate, with an average precipitation of at least 80 to 100 inches (200 to 250 centimeters) per year. Because of the great amount of precipitation, forest fires occur only rarely. As a result, trees in a rain forest are able to grow to a very large size and a very old age.

Tropical rain forests

Tropical rain forests can be found in equatorial regions of Central and South America, west-central Africa, and Southeast Asia, including New Guinea and the northeastern coast of Australia. Tropical rain forests are the most complex of the world's ecosystems in terms of both their physical structure and the tremendous biodiversity of species they support. Because they support such a wide variety and number of plants, animals, and microorganisms, tropical rain forests represent the highest peak of ecosystem development on Earth.

Productivity of tropical rain forests. Tropical rain forests have a very complex canopy, consisting of many layers of foliage (leaves) intertwined with each other. This canopy makes up one of the densest leafy surfaces found in any of Earth's ecosystems. The presence of so many leaves make it possible for tropical rain forests to capture solar energy and convert it to plant production with a high degree of efficiency.

In the tropical rain forests, woody tissues of trees account for about 80 percent of the biomass. (Biomass is the sum total of living and dead plants and animals.) Another 15 percent of the organic matter occurs in soil and litter (the uppermost, slightly decaying layer of organic matter on the forest floor), and about 5 percent is foliage. In contrast, a much larger fraction of the biomass in temperate forests occurs as organic matter in the soil and on forest floor. The reason for this difference is temperature. In tropical rain forests, dead biomass decays very rapidly because of warm and humid environmental conditions.

This fact explains a strange contradiction about tropical rain forests. In spite of the abundance of living and dead plants and animals they contain, they are very fragile environments. If trees are cut down, the vast majority of the forest's biomass is lost. In addition, the soil in tropical rain forests is generally not very fertile. When trees are removed, it is usually difficult to get other plants and crops to grow in the same place. The destruction of tropical rain forests in order to obtain land for agriculture, then, has had some surprising results. Very rich, productive stands of trees have been lost, but those stands have not been replaced by farms that are as rich. In fact, the land is often simply lost to any form of productive plant growing.

Biodiversity in tropical rain forests. An enormous number of species of plants, animals, and microorganisms occurs in tropical rain forests. In fact, this type of ecosystem accounts for a much larger fraction of Earth's biodiversity than any other category. Some scientists estimate that as many as 30 million to 50 million species may occur on Earth, and that about 90 percent of these species occur in tropical ecosystems, the great majority of those in rain forests.

Most of the undiscovered species are probably insects, especially beetles. However, tropical rain forests also contain immense numbers of undiscovered species of other arthropods (invertebrates with external skeletons), as well as many

A Kenyan rain forest.
(Reproduced by permission of The Stock Market.)

new plants and microorganisms. Even new species of birds and mammals are being discovered in tropical rain forests, further highlighting the fact that so much still is to be learned about that natural ecosystem.

Temperate rain forests

Temperate rain forests are most common on the windward sides of coastal mountain ranges. In such areas, warm, moisture-laden winds from the ocean are forced upwards over the mountains. There they cool, form clouds, and release their moisture as large quantities of rainfall. Temperate rain forests are found primarily along the west coasts of North and South America and in New Zealand.

Many types of temperate rain forests exist. In northern California, for example, coastal rain forests are often dominated by stands of enormous redwood trees more than 1,000 years old. Old-growth rain forests elsewhere on the western coast of North America are dominated by other conifer (cone-bearing) species, especially Douglas-fir, western hemlock, sitka spruce, red cedar, and fir. Rain forests also occur in wet, frost-free parts of the Southern Hemisphere adjacent to the ocean. In parts of New Zealand, for example, the most common tree species in temperate rain forests are southern beech and southern pines.

The burning of the rain forests to gain land for farming has not been successful, since rain forest soil is not very fertile. *(Reproduced by permission of National Center for Atmospheric Research.)*

Most species that are found in temperate rain forests also live in younger forests. However, some important exceptions exist. For example, in temperate rain forests of the Pacific coast of North America, the spotted owl, marbled murrelet, and some species of plants, mosses, and lichens appear to require the special conditions provided by old-growth forests and do not survive well in other ecosystems.

[*See also* **Biodiversity; Forestry; Forests**]

Where to Learn More

Books

Earth Sciences

Cox, Reg, and Neil Morris. *The Natural World.* Philadelphia, PA: Chelsea House, 2000.

Dasch, E. Julius, editor. *Earth Sciences for Students.* Four volumes. New York: Macmillan Reference, 1999.

Denecke, Edward J., Jr. *Let's Review: Earth Science.* Second edition. Hauppauge, NY: Barron's, 2001.

Engelbert, Phillis. *Dangerous Planet: The Science of Natural Disasters.* Three volumes. Farmington Hills, MI: UXL, 2001.

Gardner, Robert. *Human Evolution.* New York: Franklin Watts, 1999.

Hall, Stephen. *Exploring the Oceans.* Milwaukee, WI: Gareth Stevens, 2000.

Knapp, Brian. *Earth Science: Discovering the Secrets of the Earth.* Eight volumes. Danbury, CT: Grolier Educational, 2000.

Llewellyn, Claire. *Our Planet Earth.* New York: Scholastic Reference, 1997.

Moloney, Norah. *The Young Oxford Book of Archaeology.* New York: Oxford University Press, 1997.

Nardo, Don. *Origin of Species: Darwin's Theory of Evolution.* San Diego, CA: Lucent Books, 2001.

Silverstein, Alvin, Virginia Silverstein, and Laura Silverstein Nunn. *Weather and Climate.* Brookfield, CN: Twenty-First Century Books, 1998.

Williams, Bob, Bob Ashley, Larry Underwood, and Jack Herschbach. *Geography.* Parsippany, NJ: Dale Seymour Publications, 1997.

Life Sciences

Barrett, Paul M. *National Geographic Dinosaurs.* Washington, D.C.: National Geographic Society, 2001.

Fullick, Ann. *The Living World.* Des Plaines, IL: Heinemann Library, 1999.

Gamlin, Linda. *Eyewitness: Evolution.* New York: Dorling Kindersley, 2000.

Greenaway, Theresa. *The Plant Kingdom: A Guide to Plant Classification and Biodiversity.* Austin, TX: Raintree Steck-Vaughn, 2000.

Kidd, J. S., and Renee A Kidd. *Life Lines: The Story of the New Genetics.* New York: Facts on File, 1999.

Kinney, Karin, editor. *Our Environment.* Alexandria, VA: Time-Life Books, 2000.

Where to Learn More

Nagel, Rob. *Body by Design: From the Digestive System to the Skeleton.* Two volumes. Farmington Hills, MI: UXL., 2000.

Parker, Steve. *The Beginner's Guide to Animal Autopsy: A "Hands-in" Approach to Zoology, the World of Creatures and What's Inside Them.* Brookfield, CN: Copper Beech Books, 1997.

Pringle, Laurence. *Global Warming: The Threat of Earth's Changing Climate.* New York: SeaStar Books, 2001.

Riley, Peter. *Plant Life.* New York: Franklin Watts, 1999.

Stanley, Debbie. *Genetic Engineering: The Cloning Debate.* New York: Rosen Publishing Group, 2000.

Whyman, Kate. *The Animal Kingdom: A Guide to Vertebrate Classification and Biodiversity.* Austin, TX: Raintree Steck-Vaughn, 1999.

Physical Sciences

Allen, Jerry, and Georgiana Allen. *The Horse and the Iron Ball: A Journey Through Time, Space, and Technology.* Minneapolis, MN: Lerner Publications, 2000.

Berger, Samantha, *Light.* New York: Scholastic, 1999.

Bonnet, Bob L., and Dan Keen. *Physics.* New York: Sterling Publishing, 1999.

Clark, Stuart. *Discovering the Universe.* Milwaukee, WI: Gareth Stevens, 2000.

Fleisher, Paul, and Tim Seeley. *Matter and Energy: Basic Principles of Matter and Thermodynamics.* Minneapolis, MN: Lerner Publishing, 2001.

Gribbin, John. *Eyewitness: Time and Space.* New York: Dorling Kindersley, 2000.

Holland, Simon. *Space.* New York: Dorling Kindersley, 2001.

Kidd, J. S., and Renee A. Kidd. *Quarks and Sparks: The Story of Nuclear Power.* New York: Facts on File, 1999.

Levine, Shar, and Leslie Johnstone. *The Science of Sound and Music.* New York: Sterling Publishing, 2000

Naeye, Robert. *Signals from Space: The Chandra X-ray Observatory.* Austin, TX: Raintree Steck-Vaughn, 2001.

Newmark, Ann. *Chemistry.* New York: Dorling Kindersley, 1999.

Oxlade, Chris. *Acids and Bases.* Chicago, IL: Heinemann Library, 2001.

Vogt, Gregory L. *Deep Space Astronomy.* Brookfield, CT: Twenty-First Century Books, 1999.

Technology and Engineering Sciences

Baker, Christopher W. *Scientific Visualization: The New Eyes of Science.* Brookfield, CT: Millbrook Press, 2000.

Cobb, Allan B. *Scientifically Engineered Foods: The Debate over What's on Your Plate.* New York: Rosen Publishing Group, 2000.

Cole, Michael D. *Space Launch Disaster: When Liftoff Goes Wrong.* Springfield, NJ: Enslow, 2000.

Deedrick, Tami. *The Internet.* Austin, TX: Raintree Steck-Vaughn, 2001.

DuTemple, Leslie A. *Oil Spills.* San Diego, CA: Lucent Books, 1999.

Gaines, Ann Graham. *Satellite Communication.* Mankata, MN: Smart Apple Media, 2000.

Gardner, Robert, and Dennis Shortelle. *From Talking Drums to the Internet: An Encyclopedia of Communications Technology.* Santa Barbara, CA: ABC-Clio, 1997.

Graham, Ian S. *Radio and Television.* Austin, TX: Raintree Steck-Vaughn, 2000.

Parker, Steve. *Lasers: Now and into the Future.* Englewood Cliffs, NJ: Silver Burdett Press, 1998.

Sachs, Jessica Snyder. *The Encyclopedia of Inventions.* New York: Franklin Watts, 2001.

Wilkinson, Philip. *Building.* New York: Dorling Kindersley, 2000.

Wilson, Anthony. *Communications: How the Future Began.* New York: Larousse Kingfisher Chambers, 1999.

Periodicals

Archaeology. Published by Archaeological Institute of America, 656 Beacon Street, 4th Floor, Boston, Massachusetts 02215. Also online at www.archaeology.org.

Astronomy. Published by Kalmbach Publishing Company, 21027 Crossroads Circle, Brookfield, WI 53186. Also online at www.astronomy.com.

Discover. Published by Walt Disney Magazine, Publishing Group, 500 S. Buena Vista, Burbank, CA 91521. Also online at www.discover.com.

National Geographic. Published by National Geographic Society, 17th & M Streets, NW, Washington, DC 20036. Also online at www.nationalgeographic.com.

New Scientist. Published by New Scientist, 151 Wardour St., London, England W1F 8WE. Also online at www.newscientist.com (includes links to more than 1,600 science sites).

Popular Science. Published by Times Mirror Magazines, Inc., 2 Park Ave., New York, NY 10024. Also online at www.popsci.com.

Science. Published by American Association for the Advancement of Science, 1333 H Street, NW, Washington, DC 20005. Also online at www.sciencemag.org.

Science News. Published by Science Service, Inc., 1719 N Street, NW, Washington, DC 20036. Also online at www.sciencenews.org.

Scientific American. Published by Scientific American, Inc., 415 Madison Ave, New York, NY 10017. Also online at www.sciam.com.

Smithsonian. Published by Smithsonian Institution, Arts & Industries Bldg., 900 Jefferson Dr., Washington, DC 20560. Also online at www.smithsonianmag.com.

Weatherwise. Published by Heldref Publications, 1319 Eighteenth St., NW, Washington, DC 20036. Also online at www.weatherwise.org.

Web Sites

Cyber Anatomy (provides detailed information on eleven body systems and the special senses) *http://library.thinkquest.org/11965/*

The DNA Learning Center (provides in-depth information about genes for students and educators) *http://vector.cshl.org/*

Educational Hotlists at the Franklin Institute (provides extensive links and other resources on science subjects ranging from animals to wind energy) *http://sln.fi.edu/tfi/hotlists/hotlists.html*

ENC Web Links: Science (provides an extensive list of links to sites covering subject areas under earth and space science, physical science, life science, process skills, and the history of science) *http://www.enc.org/weblinks/science/*

ENC Web Links: Math topics (provides an extensive list of links to sites covering subject areas under topics such as advanced mathematics, algebra, geometry, data analysis and probability, applied mathematics, numbers and operations, measurement, and problem solving) *http://www.enc.org/weblinks/math/*

Encyclopaedia Britannica Discovering Dinosaurs Activity Guide *http://dinosaurs.eb.com/dinosaurs/study/*

The Exploratorium: The Museum of Science, Art, and Human Perception *http://www.exploratorium.edu/*

ExploreMath.com (provides highly interactive math activities for students and educators) *http://www.exploremath.com/*

ExploreScience.com (provides highly interactive science activities for students and educators) *http://www.explorescience.com/*

Imagine the Universe! (provides information about the universe for students aged 14 and up) *http://imagine.gsfc.nasa.gov/*

Mad Sci Network (highly searchable site provides extensive science information in addition to a search engine and a library to find science resources on the Internet; also allows students to submit questions to scientists) *http://www.madsci.org/*

The Math Forum (provides math-related information and resources for elementary through graduate-level students) *http://forum.swarthmore.edu/*

NASA Human Spaceflight: International Space Station (NASA homepage for the space station) *http://www.spaceflight.nasa.gov/station/*

NASA's Origins Program (provides up-to-the-minute information on the scientific quest to understand life and its place in the universe) *http://origins.jpl.nasa.gov/*

National Human Genome Research Institute (provides extensive information about the Human Genome Project) *http://www.nhgri.nih.gov:80/index.html*

New Scientist Online Magazine *http://www.newscientist.com/*

The Nine Planets (provides a multimedia tour of the history, mythology, and current scientific knowledge of each of the planets and moons in our solar system) *http://seds.lpl.arizona.edu/nineplanets/nineplanets/nineplanets.html*

The Particle Adventure (provides an interactive tour of quarks, neutrinos, antimatter, extra dimensions, dark matter, accelerators, and particle detectors) *http://particleadventure.org/*

PhysLink: Physics and astronomy online education and reference *http://physlink.com/*

Savage Earth Online (online version of the PBS series exploring earthquakes, volcanoes, tsunamis, and other seismic activity) *http://www.pbs.org/wnet/savageearth/*

Science at NASA (provides breaking information on astronomy, space science, earth science, and biological and physical sciences) *http://science.msfc.nasa.gov/*

Science Learning Network (provides Internet-guided science applications as well as many middle school science links) *http://www.sln.org/*

SciTech Daily Review (provides breaking science news and links to dozens of science and technology publications; also provides links to numerous "interesting" science sites) *http://www.scitechdaily.com/*

Space.com (space news, games, entertainment, and science fiction) *http://www.space.com/index.html*

SpaceDaily.com (provides latest news about space and space travel) *http://www.spacedaily.com/*

SpaceWeather.com (science news and information about the Sun-Earth environment) *http://www.spaceweather.com/*

The Why Files (exploration of the science behind the news; funded by the National Science Foundation) *http://whyfiles.org/*

Index

Italic type indicates volume numbers; **boldface** type indicates entries and their page numbers; (ill.) indicates illustrations.

A

Abacus *1:* **1-2** 1 (ill.)
Abelson, Philip *1:* 24
Abortion *3:* 565
Abrasives *1:* **2-4,** 3 (ill.)
Absolute dating *4:* 616
Absolute zero *3:* 595-596
Abyssal plains *7:* 1411
Acceleration *1:* **4-6**
Acetylsalicylic acid *1:* **6-9,** 8 (ill.)
Acheson, Edward G. *1:* 2
Acid rain *1:* **9-14,** 10 (ill.), 12 (ill.), *6:* 1163, *8:* 1553
Acidifying agents *1:* 66
Acids and bases *1:* **14-16,** *8:* 1495
Acoustics *1:* **17-23,** 17 (ill.), 20 (ill.)
Acquired immunodeficiency syndrome. *See* **AIDS (acquired immunodeficiency syndrome)**
Acrophobia *8:* 1497
Actinides *1:* **23-26,** 24 (ill.)
Acupressure *1:* 121
Acupuncture *1:* 121
Adams, John Couch *7:* 1330
Adaptation *1:* **26-32,** 29 (ill.), 30 (ill.)
Addiction *1:* **32-37,** 35 (ill.), *3:* 478
Addison's disease *5:* 801

Adena burial mounds *7:* 1300
Adenosine triphosphate *7:* 1258
ADHD *2:* 237-238
Adhesives *1:* **37-39,** 38 (ill.)
Adiabatic demagnetization *3:* 597
ADP *7:* 1258
Adrenal glands *5:* 796 (ill.)
Adrenaline *5:* 800
Aerobic respiration *9:* 1673
Aerodynamics *1:* **39-43,** 40 (ill.)
Aerosols *1:* **43-49,** 43 (ill.)
Africa *1:* **49-54,** 50 (ill.), 53 (ill.)
Afterburners *6:* 1146
Agent Orange *1:* **54-59,** 57 (ill.)
Aging and death *1:* **59-62**
Agoraphobia *8:* 1497
Agriculture *1:* **62-65,** 63, 64 (ill.), *3:*582-590, *5:* 902-903, *9:* 1743-744, *7:* 1433 (ill.)
Agrochemicals *1:* **65-69,** 67 (ill.), 68 (ill.)
Agroecosystems *2:* 302
AI. *See* **Artificial intelligence**
AIDS (acquired immunodeficiency syndrome) *1:* **70-74,** 72 (ill.), *8:* 1583, *9:* 1737
Air flow *1:* 40 (ill.)
Air masses and fronts *1:* **80-82,** 80 (ill.)
Air pollution *8:* 1552, 1558
Aircraft *1:* **74-79,** 75 (ill.), 78 (ill.)
Airfoil *1:* 41
Airplanes. *See* **Aircraft**
Airships *1:* 75

B

E

M

O

Oberon   *10:* 1954
Obesity   *4:* 716
Obsession   *7:* **1405-1407**
Obsessive-compulsive disorder   *7:* 1405
Obsessive-compulsive personality disorder   *7:* 1406
Occluded fronts   *1:* 82
Ocean   *7:* **1407-1411,** 1407 (ill.)
Ocean currents   *3:* 604-605
Ocean ridges   *7:* 1410 (ill.)
Ocean zones   *7:* **1414-1418**
Oceanic archaeology.   *See* **Nautical archaeology**
Oceanic ridges   *7:* 1409
Oceanography   *7:* **1411-1414,** 1412 (ill.), 1413 (ill.)
Octopus   *7:* 1289
Oersted, Hans Christian   *1:* 124, *4:* 760, 766, *6:* 1212
Offshore drilling   *7:* 1421
Ohio River   *7:* 1355
Ohm (O)   *4:* 738
Ohm, Georg Simon   *4:* 738
Ohm's law   *4:* 740
Oil drilling   *7:* **1418-1422,** 1420 (ill.)
Oil pollution   *7:* 1424
Oil spills   *7:* **1422-1426,** 1422 (ill.), 1425 (ill.)
Oils   *6:* 1191
Olduvai Gorge   *6:* 1058
Olfaction.   *See* **Smell**
On the Origin of Species by Means of Natural Selection   *6:* 1054
On the Structure of the Human Body   *1:* 139
O'Neill, J. A.   *6:* 1211
Onnes, Heike Kamerlingh   *10:* 1850
Oort cloud   *3:* 530
Oort, Jan   *8:* 1637
Open clusters   *9:* 1808
Open ocean biome   *2:* 299
Operant conditioning   *9:* 1658
Ophediophobia   *8:* 1497
Opiates   *1:* 32
Opium   *1:* 32, 33
Orangutans   *8:* 1572, 1574 (ill.)
Orbit   *7:* **1426-1428**
Organ of Corti   *4:* 695
Organic chemistry   *7:* **1428-1431**
Organic families   *7:* 1430
Organic farming   *7:* **1431-1434,** 1433 (ill.)
Origin of life   *4:* 702
Origins of algebra   *1:* 97
Orizaba, Pico de   *7:* 1359
Orthopedics   *7:* **1434-1436**
Oscilloscopes   *10:* 1962
Osmosis   *4:* 652, *7:* **1436-1439,** 1437 (ill.)
Osmotic pressure   *7:* 1436
Osteoarthritis   *1:* 181
Osteoporosis   *9:* 1742
Otitis media   *4:* 697
Otosclerosis   *4:* 697
Ovaries   *5:* 800
Oxbow lakes   *6:* 1160
Oxidation-reduction reactions   *7:* **1439-1442,** *9:* 1648
Oxone layer   *7:* 1452 (ill.)
Oxygen family   *7:* **1442-1450,** 1448 (ill.)
Ozone   *7:* **1450-1455,** 1452 (ill.)
Ozone depletion   *1:* 48, *8:* 1555
Ozone layer   *7:* 1451

P

Packet switching   *6:* 1124
Pain   *7:* 1336
Paleoecology   *8:* **1457-1459,** 1458 (ill.)
Paleontology   *8:* **1459-1462,** 1461 (ill.)
Paleozoic era   *5:* 990, *8:* 1461
Paleozoology   *8:* 1459
Panama Canal   *6:* 1194
Pancreas   *4:* 655, *5:* 798
Pangaea   *8:* 1534, 1536 (ill.)
Pap test   *5:* 1020
Papanicolaou, George   *5:* 1020
Paper   *8:* **1462-1467,** 1464 (ill.), 1465 (ill.), 1466 (ill.)
Papyrus   *8:* 1463
Paracelsus, Philippus Aureolus   *1:* 84
Parasites   *8:* **1467-1475,** 1471 (ill.), 1472 (ill.), 1474 (ill.)
Parasitology   *8:* 1469
Parathyroid glands   *5:* 798
Paré, Ambroise   *8:* 1580, *10:* 1855
Parkinson's disease   *1:* 62
Parsons, Charles A.   *9:* 1820
Particle accelerators   *8:* **1475-1482,**